Raised By A Narcissist

A Memoir of Survival, Healing, and Reclaiming My Voice

By
Elizabeth A Hewitt

Contents

Dedication

This book is dedicated to my father, Jonny, the most wonderful man and father.

About the Author

Lizzi A Hewitt is a survivor, writer, and advocate for mental health and emotional recovery. After years of enduring emotional abuse, family estrangement, and trauma, Lizzi worked courageously with a compassionate counsellor to overcome self-harm, depression, and the lasting effects of a deeply painful past. No longer reliant on antidepressants or coping mechanisms like cutting, she has found peace, stability, and happiness in her life.

Though the wounds of her experiences remain and the grief of losing her beloved father never fades, Lizzi has reclaimed her voice and her future. She now lives a fulfilled life surrounded by love, strength, and hard-won freedom. Through her memoir, she hopes to reach others who feel alone in their pain and remind them that healing is possible and that they are never truly alone.

Chapter 1
Life of Lies

"Some children learn very early that home is not always the safest place to be."

My parents had divorced by the time I turned seven, and in many ways, that was when my mother's behaviour towards me began to change. I was only a child, so of course I did not understand it then. I trusted what I was told. I believed what the adults around me said because that is what children do.

At that age, I did not have the words for what felt wrong. I only knew that something in our home had started to feel different. There were comments, moods, silences, and little moments that stayed with me, even if I could not explain why. I had no idea then that the things my mother said and did would one day make me question not only whether she loved me, but whether I was even worth loving at all.

I have two brothers, one older and one younger, but as time went on, it felt as though our mother took a real dislike towards me. When we were very young, I thought she treated us all the same. Maybe she did, or maybe I was just too young to notice the difference. Children do not always realise when they are being treated differently. They simply accept what is happening because, to them, that is normal.

But I did begin to feel it. Not all at once, but slowly. It was in the way she spoke to me, the way she reacted to me, and the way I always seemed to feel smaller around her. I could not have explained it properly back then. I just knew that being around her often made me feel careful, as though I had to watch myself before I even understood why.

She started turning us against our father quite quickly after he left. She would make snide comments about him and belittle him, and over time, those comments became part of the way we were expected to see him. As a child, it is very hard to know what is true when one parent is telling you who the other parent is. You do not question it straight away. You just carry it.

Later on, she told us he used to hit her and that he would not let her buy sanitary items or food. She said she used to go to the greengrocer to get food they were throwing away so she could feed us. Those are heavy things to tell children. They sit inside you, even when you do not fully understand them.

Now that I know how easily she could lie, I find it very hard to believe that version of events. We always had food for packed lunches and meals, and I do not remember going hungry when I was very young. That does not mean I knew the whole truth, of course. I was a child. But it does mean that, over time, I have had to separate what I was told from what I actually remember.

When I was six, we moved into my grandparents' holiday cottage in the same village. To us children, at first, it felt like an adventure. We used to take one of the elderly neighbours' dogs for a walk, and I remember enjoying that. There were still little moments of happiness, because children can find fun almost anywhere, even when the adults around them are not giving them much stability.

The cottage only had one bedroom, with a huge bed in it. Our mother took that room for herself, and my brothers and I slept in a cupboard-type room on a mattress on the floor. At the time, I do not think I saw it as strange. I just accepted it because that was what we had been given. But it says something, does it not, when a child learns that her place is wherever there is space left over.

After the holiday cottage, we did eventually move to a different town and into a new house when I was seven. It had three bedrooms, so in a practical sense, it should have felt like things were becoming more settled. After sleeping in such a cramped space before, having an actual bedroom should have felt exciting, and I suppose part of me did feel that. Children hold on to small bits of hope, even when they do not fully understand what is happening around them.

We moved in on Christmas Eve, and to be fair, my mother did try to make it feel special. None of the furniture had arrived yet, but I chose a bedroom, and she made me a bed on the floor with covers and put up some Christmas lights. My older brother had his own room too, while our younger brother shared our mother's room. I do not remember much else about that Christmas, only little pieces of it. The lights, the empty rooms, the feeling that maybe this new house might mean something better.

For a child, those small details can mean a lot. A few covers on the floor and some Christmas lights can feel like magic when you want so badly to believe everything is going to be all right. I think that is why the memory has stayed with me. It was one of those moments where things almost felt normal, even if they were not.

I still do not really know how she managed to get a mortgage on that house, because she did not properly work. She did the occasional cleaning job here and there, but nothing steady or long-term. As far as I know, she had not had a proper job since before she married my father. She had done bits and pieces over the years, but never anything that lasted.

As a child, I did not think too much about money or how adults paid for things. You just assume they know what they are doing. But as I got older, I started to realise how strange it was. There were always gaps in the story, little things that did not quite make sense, but in our house, asking questions never felt like something you were supposed to do.

The thing with my mother is that she always seemed to believe she should be doing something important, something like teaching or another respected job. She is clever, and over the years she has earned several degrees in different subjects, so it was not that she was not capable. She was capable. That was never the issue.

The issue was that she seemed to want the status of certain things without putting in the everyday effort that came with them. Ordinary work always seemed beneath her. When I was sixteen, I got a job in a supermarket, and they were looking for staff. I remember coming home and suggesting that she apply, thinking I was being helpful. Her answer was, "I don't want to work with people who swear and smoke."

And that was the end of that. No discussion. No real consideration. Just a reason why it was not good enough for her.

That was how things often were with my mother. She could make herself sound above something, even when everyone else was simply trying to get by. I was sixteen and already working, yet she could dismiss the same kind of work as if it was beneath her.

At the time, I probably did not have the confidence to think too deeply about it, but now I can see how much of my childhood was spent watching her expect life to bend around her, while the rest of us had to adjust ourselves to whatever mood, excuse, or version of the truth she gave us.

"A house can look like a fresh start, but that does not always mean it feels like home."

Chapter 2
Changing Moods

"When a parent's mood changes without warning, a child learns to listen for danger in the silence."

Growing up with a mother like mine was never simple. Her moods could change so quickly that it was hard to keep up with them. One minute she could be happy and laughing, and the next she would be in bed crying, with no real explanation. As a child, I never knew what had caused the change. I did not know if something had happened, if someone had upset her, or if I had somehow done something wrong without realising it.

That is a heavy thing for a child to carry. You start watching everything. Her face, her voice, the way she moves around the house, even the sound of her footsteps. I learnt very early to read the room, not because I was clever, but because I felt I had to. If she was quiet, I worried. If she was crying, I worried. If she was suddenly cheerful, I still worried, because I never knew how long it would last.

There were days when it felt as though I was the adult, even though I was only a child. I would hide my own feelings because hers always seemed bigger and more important. I did not want to make things worse. I did not want to be the reason she cried or became angry. And yet, through all of that, I still wanted her love. Of course I did. She was my mother. I wanted her warmth, her comfort, her approval, even when it always seemed just out of reach.

For the first couple of years at our new school, she did get up with us. She would make breakfast and make sure our uniforms were clean. She would walk us to school as well, although sometimes she told us to walk by ourselves. My older brother and I would walk our younger brother to his infant school first, then carry on to our junior school.

She was not always there to walk us home either, but at the time it did not really bother us. It was about a twenty-minute walk, so it did not feel too far. Children get used to things very quickly, especially when they do not know any different. If something becomes part of the routine, you just accept it.

What we did not realise was that she had asked different people on our route home to keep an eye on us. On the surface, that might sound harmless, maybe even sensible. But it did not feel that way when I was a child. One time, my brothers and I were arguing about something, as siblings do, and one of the people watching us told our mother.

We had no idea how she knew. We only found that out years later. At the time, it made me feel as though she knew everything and was somehow everywhere. That feeling stayed with me. It was not just about being watched on the way home from school. It was about feeling as if there was no space where I could simply be a child without it getting back to her.

"Control does not always arrive as shouting. Sometimes it comes dressed up as care."

Our mother did make sure we were involved in lots of clubs when we were younger. I went to Girl Guides, which I actually enjoyed. The boys went to Scouts. We also played in a band every Saturday, although that was something I did not enjoy at all.

On the outside, I suppose it could have looked like she was giving us opportunities. And maybe, in some ways, she was. But the problem was that it rarely felt like we had a choice. It was not really about what I enjoyed or what suited me. It was about what she decided was best, and once she had decided, that was usually the end of it.

My auntie gave me a violin for my seventh birthday, and I am quite sure that was my mother's idea. I never particularly enjoyed playing it. It was not an instrument I would have chosen for myself. If anyone had asked me, I would have liked to learn the piano.

But being asked was not something that happened very often. Not properly, anyway. I learnt throughout my childhood, and even into the start of adulthood, that my own preferences did not matter much. If my mother had already made up her mind, then that was what I had to go along with.

I was manipulated for so much of my life that, for a long time, I did not even know how to fight against it. I felt powerless, as though every choice I made could somehow be turned into something wrong. My mother had a way of twisting things until I felt guilty, even when I had done nothing bad. If I wanted something she did not approve of, and to be honest, she disapproved of most things, I would end up feeling ashamed for wanting it in the first place.

Her disapproval did not always come through shouting. Sometimes it was just a look. Sometimes it was silence. Sometimes it was a sigh that made me feel as though I had ruined everything. Those small things might not sound like much to some people, but when you grow up with them every day, they get inside you. You start questioning yourself before anyone else even has the chance to.

Even now, writing this book, I still feel guilt at times. That is hard to admit, but it is true. Part of me still feels as though I am doing something wrong by telling the truth. But this is my truth. These are my memories, my hurt, and my life. For so many years, I was made to feel as though my voice did not matter. I do not want to live like that anymore.

"When a child makes a mistake, they need guidance. They do not need to be made to feel disposable."

That guilt followed me into almost everything, even the things most children would have simply been told off for and then allowed to learn from. But in our house, mistakes did not always feel like mistakes. They felt like proof that I was bad, difficult, or not worth keeping.

Things became worse for me when I was caught stealing sweets at eleven years old. I had become friends with a girl who was fourteen, and looking back, she was clearly already being watched by shop security. I did not understand that at the time. I was just a child, trying to fit in with someone older than me.

One day, when I went to the shop with her, she stuffed a load of sweets down my coat. We were stopped by security on the way out, and the police were called. I knew I had done something wrong by being involved, but I also remember feeling terrified more than anything else. Not terrified of the police, really, but of what would happen when my mother found out.

I lied to the police at first because I was so frightened of my mother's reaction. Eventually, they got me to tell the truth, and then they rang her. She came to collect me, and I remember the dread of going home with her. That feeling of sitting beside her, knowing I had upset her, knowing there would be consequences, was awful.

As soon as we got home, she told me she had called my auntie, my dad's sister, and that she was coming to pick me up. She said I could go and live with my dad because she did not want me around anymore. Then she told me to go and pack my bags.

I was only eleven. I had done something wrong, yes, but I was still a child. What I needed was to be corrected, spoken to, and helped to understand. Instead, I was made to feel as though one mistake meant I could be thrown away.

Even now, I do not know if she was serious. I assume she was not, because nothing came of it. No one came to collect me. I did not go to my dad's. It was most likely just another way to frighten me and make me feel unwanted.

At the time, I burst into tears and begged her not to make me go. That is the heartbreaking part, really. I was begging to stay in a place where I did not feel properly loved, because it was all I knew. A child will still cling to the parent who hurts them, because the need to be loved by your mother does not just disappear.

Now, when I think about it, part of me wishes she had meant it. I wish she had called my auntie. I wish someone had come and taken me to my dad. I truly believe my upbringing would have been very different if that had happened. Maybe I would have felt safe. Maybe I would have been allowed to be a child.

"The pain was bad enough, but being told to hide the truth made it worse."

She had never treated me especially well before that, but after the incident with the sweets, it felt worse. Still, there were other things that had already shown me where I stood, even before then. One of those memories is from when I was ten years old.

My uncle made a tent outside against the barn in our garden. It was not really a proper tent. He had put a sheet up against the wall, and that became a little camping spot for my younger brother and me. We loved camping outside, so to us it felt exciting. Children do not always notice danger when something feels like an adventure.

The problem was that the barn was unsafe. Very unsafe. I do not think we understood that properly. We trusted the adults around us to know what was safe and what was not. That is what children do.

Partway through the night, I woke up in the most frightening way. A brick, or possibly more than one, had come loose from the top of the barn and fallen onto me. One landed on my face. I screamed. It was not just a little cry. It was the sort of scream that comes out of you before you even know what has happened.

My mother later told me that two bricks had fallen, one on my face and one on my chest. She said the one on my chest did no damage because I had my teddy panda there, and that otherwise it could have killed me. I do not know if that part is true. It may have been. It may also have been another one of her versions of events, because she was not actually with us when it happened.

What I do remember clearly is the fear, the pain, and the blood. I remember being a little girl who had been hurt badly enough to scream, and I remember what my mother seemed most concerned about.

Our mother came out after hearing the noise. I had blood all over my face, but her first concern did not seem to be me. She was worried about whether the neighbours had heard me scream. She was worried they might call the council or the police. She was worried that someone would make her take the barn down because it was unsafe.

She complained that she would not be able to sell the house without the barn.

I was ten years old, bleeding and frightened, and somehow the barn mattered more. The house mattered more. What other people might think mattered more. I cannot explain how that feels to a child, except to say that it teaches you very quickly that your pain is not the most important thing in the room.

She did eventually clean me up, but she did not take me to the hospital. Of course, if she had taken me there, questions might have been asked. Someone might have wanted to know how it had happened. Someone might have said the barn was dangerous.

So, I was kept at home. I was patched up, but I was not properly checked. I was hurt, but the truth of how I had been hurt had to be managed. That was something I became used to, not just being hurt, but being expected to protect the person who should have been protecting me.

This happened on a Saturday night, so by Monday I had to go to school. Before we left, she had put fresh plasters over my wounds and gave me a talking-to about what I was allowed to say. I was told not to tell anyone what had really happened. Instead, I had to say that a tent pole had fallen on my face.

Of course, she came into school herself and told the teachers the same story. That way, the lie was already in place before anyone could ask me properly. I only dared to tell my best friend the truth.

I think about that now and feel sad for the little girl I was. Not only had I been injured, but I had also been taught to cover it up. I had to carry the pain on my face and the truth in my chest, knowing I was not allowed to say what had really happened. That is a lot for any child. It was not just the bricks that hurt me. It was the message that came afterwards: stay quiet, protect her, and do not make trouble.

Chapter 3
Our Dad Never Stood A Chance

"When a child is made to choose between two parents, love starts to feel like something they have to hide."

We did see our father at first. It started as every other weekend, and the three of us would go together. Those visits meant a lot to us, even if I did not fully understand at the time how fragile they were. To me, he was just my dad, and seeing him felt normal, comforting, and happy.

Then, somewhere along the way, when I was about nine years old, our mother decided that the visits should change. Instead of all three of us going together, she split us up. My older brother was sent on his own for just the Saturday, while my younger brother and I stayed for the weekend. I did not know why it had to be that way. I only knew that something which had once felt simple was slowly being made more complicated.

After that, the visits became once a month for each of us, but on different weekends. It felt as though we were being separated piece by piece, not all at once, but enough to notice. Then, when I was about nine, we were told that we could no longer call our dad "Dad". We had to call him by his first name, even to his face.

That might sound like a small thing to someone who has never been put in that position, but to a child, it was huge. He was my dad. That was what he had always been to me. Being told not to call him that felt wrong in a way I could not explain.

I knew I was not going to call him by his name. I could not do that to him. Even at nine years old, I understood that it would hurt him. I could imagine the look on his face, and I could not bear the thought of causing him that pain.

But I could not call him Dad either, because disobeying my mother filled me with guilt. That was the hold she had over me. So I ended up saying neither. I avoided calling him anything at all. It is sad to think about that now, a little girl stuck between wanting to love her father openly and being too afraid to go against her mother.

I do not know if my brothers did what our mother told us to do or not. I only know what it felt like for me. I loved my dad so much, and I loved visiting him. My brothers enjoyed those visits too. They were happy times, which perhaps made everything even harder.

He would make us pancakes for breakfast, and he would shape them for us. My brother's would be a dinosaur, and mine would be a bear. It was such a simple thing, but it stayed with me because it felt loving. It felt like effort. It felt like he saw us as children worth making happy.

"Some choices were never really choices. They were traps dressed up as tests."

One night, our mother told my younger brother and me that we had to run away while everyone was asleep. Our dad lived on the outskirts of the village, and she told us we were to leave his house, walk into the village, find a telephone box, ring her, and then she would come and pick us up.

I cannot imagine putting that kind of fear into children now. We were far too young to be told to do something like that. We were supposed to be safe in bed, not lying there trying to decide whether we should sneak out into the dark because our mother had told us to.

My brother and I sat in our room for ages, whispering about whether we should do it. Everyone had gone to bed. The house was quiet, and outside was completely dark. I remember feeling frightened, not just of leaving, but of staying.

I was only nine or ten, and my younger brother was only seven or eight. We were children. We should never have been put in that position. The silence in the house felt so heavy, and all I could hear was my own heart pounding. We did not dare move, but we were also scared of what would happen if we did not do what she had told us to do.

Our dad would have been terrified if he had woken up and found us gone. I have no doubt that our mother would have used it against him somehow. That was the worst part. Even as a child, I could sense that this was not really about us. It felt like we were being used in something much bigger than we could understand.

I was shaking at the thought of running away, but I was also scared of what our mother would say if we did not. There was no right choice. If we went, we would hurt and frighten our dad. If we stayed, we risked angering our mother. It was one of her games, and like so many of them, we were never meant to win.

On one of our earlier visits, back when the three of us still went together, my dad's Land Rover got a flat tyre while he was driving us home. This was before mobile phones, so he sent my older brother to a telephone box to ring our mother and let her know what had happened.

It should have been nothing more than that. A flat tyre. A delay. Something ordinary. My dad dealt with it as any parent would. He changed the tyre, made sure our mother had been told, and then got us back on the road.

But when we arrived home, there was a police officer standing there, talking to our mother. She had rung the police to say that my dad had not brought us back.

My dad explained that the Land Rover had got a flat tyre and that he had sent my older brother to ring her from the telephone box to say we would be late. The officer listened, then just shook his head and walked off. I was young, but even I could feel how unnecessary it all was.

It was embarrassing and upsetting, although I do not think I had the words for that then. I only knew that something normal had been turned into something serious, and somehow my dad was the one left having to explain himself.

That was one of many times we watched her turn something ordinary into something dramatic. A simple delay became a police matter. A visit with our dad became another reason for tension. Everything seemed to carry a hidden meaning, and as children, we could feel it, even when we could not explain it.

It was like living inside a story someone else was writing for us. We were the children in the middle, pulled into fear, guilt, and confusion, while the adults around us made decisions that changed the shape of our lives. We never knew what the ending would be. We only knew that our dad was slowly being pushed further away from us, and none of us had the power to stop it.

That sense of being caught in the middle did not end with the police at the door. It carried on in quieter, heavier ways. Our dad was still our dad, but bit by bit, it felt as though loving him was being made into something we had to feel guilty about.

"Sometimes a child's silence is not agreement. Sometimes it is fear."

She never hit me, but she did not need to. She had other ways of getting me to do what she wanted. Guilt was one of them. Fear was another. From a very young age, I had been taught to think about her feelings before my own, to worry about upsetting her, and to feel responsible for things no child should have carried.

Even now, as an adult, I still catch myself feeling guilty over things I have no control over. That does not come from nowhere. It comes from years of being made to feel that my choices, my feelings, and even my love for my dad were somehow a betrayal of her.

One time, when I was about eight or nine years old, she decided to take us to court. There would be a judge there, and our father too, because they were discussing the visiting arrangements. I did not really understand what court meant at that age. I only knew it sounded serious, and I knew my mother had already made it clear what she expected from us.

When we arrived, a mediator took my older brother into a room to speak to him. After that, she came back for my younger brother and me to ask us our thoughts about visiting our dad. It should have been a chance for us to speak honestly, but it was not that simple. We had already been told what we were supposed to say.

The night before, our mother had sat the three of us down and told us what to say to the judge. None of it was kind. None of it sounded like the dad I knew and loved. It was all awful, and it was all lies.

She wanted me to say that my dad treated me like a rag doll. I can still feel how wrong that sounded, even now. Those were not my words. They were hers. She was trying to put them into my mouth and make me carry them as if they belonged to me.

When we went into the courtroom, the judge eventually asked the three of us to stand. Then he asked us directly what we thought about visiting our dad. Not one of us said a word.

We did not look at our parents. We did not speak. We just stood there, frozen. I think people sometimes forget that silence from a child does not always mean they have nothing to say. Sometimes it means they are terrified of the consequences.

I could not say those lies in front of a judge. I could not say them in front of my dad either. I just wanted to cry. I wanted the whole thing to be over. I wanted someone to understand without me having to say anything.

The judge let us sit back down, but when we got outside, our mother was furious. She was angry because we had not said what she told us to say.

That is the part that stayed with me. She was not relieved that we had not lied. She was not concerned that we had been frightened. She was angry because we had not performed the story she had prepared for us.

The last time I saw my dad as a child, I was ten years old. I did not know it was going to be the last time. Children never know when something ordinary is about to become a memory they will spend years trying to understand.

At the time, I did not know what had really happened. I only found out the truth many years later, after speaking to my auntie, my dad's sister.

Back when I was ten, our mother told my younger brother and me to pack our overnight things. Pyjamas, a teddy, and a snack, just like we normally did when we were going to stay with our dad. Then she sent us outside to wait for him to pick us up.

So we waited. Two children standing outside with our little bags, expecting our dad to arrive. But he did not come.

She was watching from inside the house while we waited. We waited for ages. Then she came out and told us he obviously was not coming, so we went back inside. After that, the visits stopped. Just like that. No proper explanation. No goodbye. No chance to understand.

According to our mother, my older brother had told our dad, when he came to pick him up, that he did not want to visit anymore. That was the story we were given. As children, we had no way of knowing whether it was true. We only had what she told us, and by then, she had already spent years shaping what we were allowed to believe.

"The truth did not give me back those lost years, but it finally explained why they were taken."

Years later, my auntie told me that another court case had taken place. A judge had told my father that he needed to stop the visits because they were causing too many problems for our mother's mental health and state of mind.

Every time my brothers and I came back from seeing our dad, we were happy. We would talk about the lovely time we had had with him, and somehow that was seen as a risk. Not a risk because of him, but because of how our happiness affected her.

The judge said that if we carried on seeing our father, our mother might need to be admitted to hospital for psychiatric care, and there would be nowhere for the three of us to go. The social worker had apparently said she was reasonably happy that we were being looked after well enough the rest of the time, so the visits had to stop in our best interests.

I still find that painful to think about. Our best interests somehow meant losing the parent who made us feel loved, safe, and wanted. Our best interests meant staying in a home where fear, guilt, and control were already shaping who I was becoming.

To me, this shows just how much control our mother had over the situation. Our father was devastated. He lost so much more than visits. He lost years with his children, years that none of us could ever get back.

I do not think I will ever be able to fully forgive my mother for this part in particular. My dad passed away without ever seeing either of his sons again, and that is something I find almost impossible to accept.

He did try over the years when we were young, but his representative told him that, for the time being, nothing could be done. So, in the end, he waited. He hoped that one day, one of us, or maybe all three of us, would get in touch.

That thought breaks my heart. While I was growing up believing he had not come for us, he was somewhere else hoping we would come back to him.

Out of everything my mother did, this is, and always will be, one of my saddest memories. In the letter I later received from her, she wrote that our dad had all the chances to contact us but clearly was not interested.

But after learning the truth from my auntie, I know that was another lie. He was interested. He did care. He had not walked away because he did not love us. The situation had been taken out of his hands, and we were left believing something that hurt all of us.

No matter how many years have passed, the ache of that loss still finds me in quiet moments. It is the kind of sadness that sits deep inside you, because now I know my dad waited for us. He hoped for us. He wanted us. And he died without ever getting the chance to hold his sons again.

There is a pain in that truth that time has not really softened. I often wonder what he thought in those last years. I wonder if he blamed himself. I wonder if he still pictured our faces the way we were when we were little. I wonder if he felt forgotten.

The guilt of not knowing the truth sooner, of not being able to reach him, still feels heavy sometimes. I know I was only a child. I know it was not my fault. But grief does not always listen to reason.

It was never supposed to end like that. None of it was.

Chapter 4
Bullies & Lies

After everything that happened with our dad, it felt as though even our name was no longer allowed to belong to him. Little by little, parts of him were being removed from our lives, and our surname was one of them.

"A name should feel like belonging, not another thing a child is made to lose."

Our mother changed our surnames from our father's name to her maiden name when I was twelve. It was not done legally at the time, because she would have needed our father's consent for that. But at school, she changed it anyway, and that became the name everyone used for us.

At that age, I did not understand the legal side of it. I only knew that another part of my dad was being taken away from me. His name was part of who I was, and suddenly it felt as though even that had to be hidden or replaced. Then, when each of us turned eighteen, she made us change our surname legally as well.

I did not understand then how much a name could matter. Children do not sit and think about identity in a grown-up way. They simply feel when something has changed. They feel the loss before they have the words for it.

For me, it was not only about a surname. It was about belonging. One name connected me to my dad, and the other was something my mother had chosen for us. I was too young to challenge it, so I went along with it. But I think a part of me always knew that something had been taken from me.

I have actually changed my surname four times, and I have only been married once. After my mother threw me out, I changed my name back to my dad's surname, which was my birth name. Later, I changed it again when I got married.

It might sound like a small detail, but names carry so much. They hold family, history, belonging, and identity. For me, my surname was never just a surname. It became another reminder of how much had been decided for me before I was old enough to decide anything for myself.

"Sometimes the bullies at school are not the ones who leave the deepest marks."

I was bullied a lot at secondary school, but honestly, those children were the least of my problems. That may sound strange, because bullying can be awful, and it was. But by then, I was already used to feeling small, unwanted, and not properly protected.

I never told my mother about the bullies because I could not see the point. I did not believe she would help me in the way I needed. Part of me probably thought she would dismiss it, twist it, or somehow make me feel worse. So I kept it to myself, just as I kept so many other things to myself.

Years later, when I was about twenty-three, I did tell her that I had been bullied at school. Her response was not comfort. It was not sadness for what I had gone through. Instead, she said, "I didn't have time to pay attention to you because your little brother was coming home aged fourteen in tears because of bullies, and I had to hug him to sleep because you know what kids that age can do."

The way she said it made it sound as though he had been in a very dark place, possibly even suicidal. And once again, my pain was pushed aside. It was as if there was no room for what had happened to me because someone else's story had to be bigger.

It turned out that was not true. When I later moved in with my younger brother, I happened to mention bullying at school. He told me he had not really been bullied because he spent most of his time in the library with his friends.

When I told him what our mother had said, he just laughed and said it never happened.

That stayed with me. Not because I blamed him, of course I did not. But because it showed me, again, how easily she could create a story and make it sound real. She could take something that never happened and use it to explain why she had not been there for me. That was the part that hurt.

It also made me question other things she had told me over the years. Once you realise one story has been made up, it is difficult not to look back at everything else and wonder what else had been changed, exaggerated, or twisted. That is a very unsettling feeling, especially when those stories shaped how I understood my own childhood.

When I started secondary school, my mother was actually lovely. She got me a new school bag, a new uniform, a pencil case, a calculator, and everything else I needed. She laid it all out on the sofa for me with a card.

I remember how much that meant to me. It felt special. It felt thoughtful. It was one of those rare moments when I felt as though she genuinely cared. And because those moments were so rare, I held on to them tightly.

That is what made things so confusing. If she had been cruel all the time, maybe it would have been easier to understand. But she was not. Sometimes she could be thoughtful. Sometimes she could make me feel special. Those moments made me hope that maybe things were changing, or that maybe I had finally done something right.

She had even got out of bed, which later became something I could barely remember happening, because that habit did not last through those school years. Her kindness was rare, but whenever it appeared, I was happy. I loved her each time she was nice to me.

That is what people do not always understand. I did not stop wanting my mother just because she hurt me. I still wanted her love. I still wanted her approval. I still wanted those softer moments to be real and lasting.

But the kindness never stayed for long. It was like being given just enough warmth to keep wanting more. I think that is why I kept loving her so much, even when she hurt me. I was always waiting for that version of her to come back.

Chapter 5
No Structure

After the confusion of school, names, bullies, and those rare moments when my mother could almost seem caring, home still never felt steady. There were times when it looked like she was doing the right things from the outside, but inside the house, there was very little structure, comfort, or proper care.

"When there is no routine, a child learns to live around the chaos instead of being protected from it."

We were never really given a bedtime. We just went to bed whenever we wanted, which sounds fun when you are a child, but it also meant there was very little routine. No real sense of being tucked in, settled down, or looked after in that normal way children need.

My younger brother and I shared a bedroom, whilst our older brother had his own smaller room. We had a bunk bed, which I did love. I chose the top bunk, and my brother was happy with that. That part of it felt ordinary enough, even nice in its own way. It was one of those small childhood things I could enjoy, even though the bigger picture around us was far from normal.

As far as I can remember, our mother never really cleaned our bedrooms. At first, that did not affect me too much because I was quite a clean child. My younger brother was not the same, and he was much messier. In that way, he took after our mother more than I did.

Over time, she seemed to give up on cleaning the house altogether. I cannot remember one clear moment when it started. It was not as though the house changed overnight. It happened slowly, little by little. More things appeared. More things stayed where they were left. Broken items, old items, things most people would have thrown away, all began to gather around us.

As a child, you do not always understand that a house is becoming unmanageable. You just live in it. You step around things. You get used to smells, mess, clutter, and corners of rooms that no longer feel usable. It becomes normal because it is all you know.

She was definitely a hoarder, and it became much worse over time. She would keep things most people would have thrown away once they were finished with or broken. To her, everything seemed to have a possible use one day, even if that day never came.

She even kept old mattresses in case she needed them later, because she wanted to adopt children. Not just one or two, either, but five or six at a time. I remember finding that strange, even then. The house was already chaotic, crowded, and not properly cared for, yet she seemed to believe she could bring more children into it.

She actually went through the adoption process, but thankfully, they decided the house was not in a fit state to bring children into. I would have been about sixteen or seventeen at the time. The old mattresses she had saved were kept in the crumbling barn, which says a lot on its own.

I felt relieved when it did not happen. That might sound harsh, but I knew what it was like to grow up in that house. I knew what it felt like to need care and not properly receive it. The thought of more children coming into that environment, especially children who may already have been through trauma, worried me deeply.

From my own experience, I knew she would not have been good for those children in the long run. They would have needed patience, love, safety, and proper care. Maybe she could have been kind to them at first, especially when they were young and dependent on her. That was when she seemed to like children most, when they needed her and made her feel important.

But children grow up. They become their own people. They have opinions, feelings, and needs that are not always convenient. I knew, because I had lived it, that once those children started growing and needing more than she wanted to give, things would most likely have changed for them too.

"Neglect is not always loud. Sometimes it is a child quietly learning to take care of herself too soon."

When I was eleven, she stopped doing certain things for me because, apparently, I did not need her anymore. That was how it felt, anyway. As though reaching a certain age meant I should suddenly know how to look after myself without being taught.

She seemed to have a real problem with me getting older, which is strange because that is what children are supposed to do. They grow. But I think she liked the needy stage, the part where a child depends on you completely and makes you feel wanted. Once I began to grow into my own person, even slightly, it felt as though she pulled away.

The sad thing is, I was still a child. I was not grown up. I still needed her. I still needed guidance, care, affection, and simple everyday help. I needed a mother, not someone who decided I was suddenly old enough to be left to work things out alone.

She no longer washed my clothes, and I had to ask my younger brother how to use the washing machine. That is embarrassing to admit, but it is the truth. I was not taught properly. I was just expected to know.

I was never really taught about hygiene either. It took my grandmother asking me one day if I had any deodorant for me to realise there was a problem. Clearly, I smelled. I can still feel the shame of that. Not because my grandmother was cruel, because she was not, but because I should not have had to learn something so basic in such a humiliating way.

Children rely on adults to teach them these things. Washing clothes, looking after their bodies, understanding what they need as they grow. When nobody teaches you, you do not just magically know. You end up feeling dirty, embarrassed, and somehow at fault for something that was never properly explained to you.

When I started my period at twelve, my mother told me nothing. I went into her bedroom, where she was lying in bed, and told her what had happened. Her response was simply, "Get a tampon out of my drawer."

That was it. No comfort. No explanation. No gentle conversation to tell me I was all right and that this was normal. I had just started my period, something that can feel frightening and confusing for a young girl, and I was left to deal with it on my own.

I had no idea what to do with the tampon, and it was too large for me anyway. I was a very small twelve-year-old. She gave me no explanation at all. Thankfully, I had learnt a little bit about periods at school, so I at least knew what was happening to my body, but knowing the basics is not the same as being cared for through it.

I needed kindness in that moment. I needed someone to sit with me, explain things properly, and make me feel less ashamed. Instead, it became another moment where I had to work things out by myself.

Considering my mother had always said my father never allowed her to buy sanitary products, it shocks me that she did something so similar to her own daughter. I do not believe my dad would have denied her those things, but that was the story she told us.

She told me she used to fold up toilet paper and place it in her underwear, and that became what I had to do too, because she did not provide me with proper period products. It was such a degrading experience. There is already enough embarrassment around growing up and changing as a young girl, but having to manage it like that made me feel even smaller.

It was not just about sanitary products. It was about dignity. It was about being seen as a young girl who needed care. I did not need luxury. I needed basic things. I needed someone to notice that I still needed looking after.

For school non-uniform days, she would not even give me the £1 to take part, so I had to go to school in my uniform. It was embarrassing because everyone noticed things like that at school. Children always do.

In a strange way, though, it was sometimes a blessing in disguise, because my normal clothes would have made me a target for even more bullying. That is a horrible thing to realise, that wearing school uniform on a day when everyone else was dressed differently felt safer than wearing my own clothes.

So much of that time was spent trying not to stand out for the wrong reasons. Trying not to smell. Trying not to look neglected. Trying not to let anyone see how little help I was getting at home. It is exhausting to be a child and already feel responsible for hiding the ways you are not being cared for.

"When everything becomes a test, a child forgets what it feels like to simply enjoy something."

The lack of care at home did not only show in the house, the clothes, or the basic things I was left to work out by myself. It also showed in the pressure placed on me. Things that should have been mine to enjoy, or at least choose for myself, often became another way for my mother to push, compare, or take over.

I played the violin at grade level, but my mother wanted me to skip grade two and go straight to grade three. It was a mistake. I was not ready, and I did not have the practice time I needed. I only scored 100 points, which was just enough to pass.

To some people, passing might sound like enough, but it did not feel like that to me. It felt as though I had failed, even though I had been pushed into something too soon. I had been set up to struggle, and then I was left to carry the disappointment as if it was mine alone.

I went to school afterwards and ended up crying on the walk because I felt so disappointed in myself. I can still remember that feeling, walking along with tears coming down my face, blaming myself for not doing better.

The sad thing is, I was not really the one who had made that choice. My mother had pushed me into it. I was clearly not ready for grade three, but that did not seem to matter to her. What mattered was what she wanted me to do, not whether I felt confident, prepared, or happy.

She never seemed to care much about what I did or did not want to do. She even got herself a violin, and it felt as though that was another way to make me feel small, as if I had to measure myself against her too.

Everything seemed to become a competition, but not the kind that encouraged me. It was the kind that made me feel embarrassed, not good enough, and constantly aware that I was being compared. A mother should be the person cheering you on, not the person making you feel as though you are losing before you have even begun.

Later, I needed to take an adult class for GCSE maths because I had not done well at school or college, and I needed a C or above for university. Of course, my mother had to come with me. There was no real need for her to do the class because she was much better at maths than I was, and she was already clever enough.

But it felt as though she came along to prove something. Not to support me, but to show how clever she was. That made it harder for me. I already felt insecure about maths, and instead of feeling encouraged, I felt overshadowed. It was another situation where something that should have been about helping me move forward became about her.

When we stopped visiting our father, our mother had us join a Saturday morning orchestra. I did not enjoy it. I was shy, quiet, and did not make friends easily. I found it difficult to relax around other children, especially children who seemed confident and comfortable in themselves.

I must admit, I was jealous of the other children there. They seemed to come from loving homes. Maybe I did not know that for certain, but that was how it looked to me. They seemed lighter somehow, less worried, less guarded. I felt different from them, and because of that, I did not really want to be friends with most of them. It was easier to stay separate than to feel the gap between their lives and mine.

There was one girl I did become quite close to, and I think that mattered more than I realised at the time. When you feel lonely, even one kind person can make a place feel a little less awful.

There was also a small group of girls who were not very nice. I do not know what it is about some children, but some can be cruel without any real reason. I had not done anything to them. I was just shy and quiet, and sometimes that seems to be enough for people to pick on you.

By then, I had already learnt to make myself smaller. At home, I tried not to upset my mother. At school, I tried not to draw attention to myself. In the orchestra, I did the same. I sat there feeling awkward, watching other children seem so at ease, and wondering what was wrong with me.

The truth is, there was nothing wrong with me. I was a child who had not been given the confidence, care, or safety I needed. But I did not know that then. I only knew that I felt out of place almost everywhere, and that feeling followed me for a very long time.

Still those years feel like a blur of trying to manage things I was far too young to manage. The house, the mess, my clothes, my body, school, music, other children, my mother's moods; it all seemed to fall around me in pieces, and somehow I was expected to just cope with it.

I did not know then that I was being neglected. I did not have a name for it. I just thought this was how life was. I thought other children must somehow know things I did not, or have something in them that made them more confident, cleaner, easier to like. I did not understand that they had probably been taught, helped, cared for, and reassured in ways I had not.

All I knew was that I felt different. I felt behind. I felt embarrassed by things I should never have had to feel embarrassed about. I was still a child, but in so many ways, I had already started looking after myself. Not because I was ready, but because no one else was doing it properly.

And the saddest part is that I still wanted my mother. Even with all of it, I still wanted her to notice me, to help me, to be proud of me, to make me feel safe. I kept hoping for the version of her that appeared now and then, the one who could be kind for a little while. But most of the time, I was left trying to find my way through a life that felt messy, lonely, and far too heavy for a child to carry.

Chapter 6
Kicked Out of My Bedroom

After years of feeling out of place in my own home, I think part of me still hoped there would be one small corner that belonged to me. A bedroom is supposed to be that place for a child. It is where you keep your things, where you sleep, where you cry quietly if you need to, and where you can close the door for a little bit of peace. But even that was not something I was allowed to keep for long.

"A child should never have to feel like there is no room for them in their own home."

When I was thirteen, I was kicked out of the bedroom I shared with my younger brother because I was considered too old to share with him. I can understand that, in a normal situation, it might have made sense for me to have my own space. But that is not what happened. Instead of my brothers sharing a room, I was the one who ended up without a bedroom at all.

It was not explained to me in a way that made me feel cared for or considered. It was just decided. Once again, I was the one expected to adjust, to make myself smaller, to fit wherever there was space left.

My mother told me she could not make my brothers share because my older brother had an awful temper and could actually kill my younger brother if he was provoked enough. I know for a fact that this was not true. My older brother was, and still is, one of the most relaxed people I know. He is very much like our dad in that way.

It was another story that did not match the person I knew, but by then I was used to explanations that did not quite make sense. They were not really explanations. They were reasons given so I would accept what had already been decided.

I had to pack my things into bin bags and move up to the crowded loft. There was only just enough room for a mattress and the bags I had packed. That was it. I could not unpack anything because there was nowhere to put anything. So I lived out of those bags, which somehow made it feel even less like I had a proper place in the house.

The loft was dusty and dark, with a low ceiling that made it feel more like a storage space than a bedroom. It was not somewhere a child should have had to sleep. I remember feeling as though I had been put away, like something inconvenient that no one knew what to do with. Hidden out of sight. Forgotten.

It is hard to explain what that does to you at that age. You are already trying to understand who you are, where you belong, and whether you matter. Then you are physically moved into a space that tells you, without words, that you do not really have a place.

I slept in that cramped, stifling loft for about half the year, trying to ignore how unwanted I felt. I do not think I would have said it like that back then. I probably would have just said I was fine, because that is what I was used to doing. But I was not fine. I felt pushed out.

Then winter came, and the loft became unbearably cold because there was no insulation. I had to move downstairs and sleep on the sofa, although downstairs was not much warmer. There was never any real comfort, only this constant feeling of being moved from one unsuitable place to another.

I did not belong anywhere in that house. Even the places I slept reminded me of that.

I used to sleep in my school uniform so I would not be as cold when I got up in the morning. The collar of my white school shirt became black with dirt. I knew it looked bad, and I was deeply embarrassed by it.

When I had to get changed for P.E., I would try to hide it so the other children would not see. Children can be the cruellest, especially when they notice something that makes you different. I was already trying so hard not to stand out, but neglect has a way of showing itself, even when a child does everything they can to hide it.

"Sometimes the softest comfort came from the animals, because they asked for nothing and stayed anyway."

Our cat used to join me in the loft, and I was so grateful for him. We had been given him by an American family from the village we had lived in before. They were friends of ours, but they were moving back to America and could not take him with them.

I loved him so much. Having him there made the loft feel a little less lonely. He did not fix anything, of course, but his company mattered. Sometimes an animal can make a child feel less forgotten simply by choosing to sit beside them.

I have always found it strange that my mother seemed to love the pets we had more easily than the children she had. She could show care and affection to animals in a way that often seemed missing with me. I do not say that because I resented the animals. I loved them too. But it was painful to notice that gentleness could exist in her, just not always for me.

Eventually, I got my old bedroom back when my older brother left home to go to university, as he was doing a long course. At one point, my mother said she was going to convert the loft into a bedroom and asked if I would like it. I said yes. Then she changed her mind and gave it to my younger brother instead.

It was not even surprising by then, but it still hurt. I had learnt not to expect too much, yet somehow I still felt disappointed when something was offered and then taken away.

We had pets from the time I was about five. We started with hamsters, then we were given our cat. We also had two rabbits. When I was fourteen, our cat died of old age, and I was heartbroken.

He had been more than just a pet to me. He had been company in a house where I often felt alone. Losing him felt like losing one of the few steady comforts I had.

When I was seventeen, we were coming back from visiting our grandparents and came across two kittens on the road. They were perfectly fine, just walking about. We stopped and picked them up, and my mother drove to some farmhouses nearby to ask if they belonged to anyone. We were told to just take them, so we did.

I loved having those two little kittens around. They brought life into the house, and I loved animals, so of course I enjoyed them. But a year later, because they had not been spayed, they both had kittens a week apart. One had three, and the other had five.

At the time, I loved the kittens because they were tiny and sweet, and I was young enough to feel excited by them. But I did not think our mother would keep them all. Most people would not have done.

But she did keep them all, which meant we had ten cats in the house. Ten cats, along with all the things my mother was already collecting. It was a lot. Too much, really.

What should have been love for animals became another part of the chaos. The house was already crowded and difficult to live in, and now there were more animals, more mess, and more responsibility that was not properly managed. As much as I loved them, I could still feel how overwhelming it all was.

"Sometimes cleaning was not really about the mess. It was about wanting one small part of life to feel manageable."

With so many animals, so much clutter, and so little routine, the house could become overwhelming very quickly. There were times when I could not stand it anymore, especially the kitchen. It was the one room that should have felt clean and usable, but most of the time, it did not.

A couple of times over the years, I decided I needed to clean the kitchen myself. It would take me about eight hours, which sounds ridiculous because the kitchen was not even big. But it was filthy, so it took that long.

There were pans on the cooker with mouldy leftover food in them, mouse droppings in the cupboards, and piles of cutlery, plates, and bowls that nobody had bothered to wash. It was not just untidy. It was dirty in a way that made the whole house feel neglected.

I think part of me cleaned because I wanted to feel some control over something. If I could not make the house feel like a proper home, maybe I could at least make one room look better for a little while.

My younger brother was the worst for leaving mould-covered plates and other things in his room. When they eventually got brought downstairs and dumped in the kitchen, it just added to everything already there.

It felt never-ending. No matter how much was cleaned, more mess always seemed to appear. It was like trying to empty water from a sinking boat while everyone else kept making holes in it.

I did enjoy cleaning, especially afterwards, when the room finally looked better. There was a strange comfort in seeing a clear worktop or an empty sink. It made things feel lighter, even if only for a short time.

But it soon became frustrating because I never got any thanks, and nobody made any effort to keep it clean. Everyone just carried on as they had before, piling plates into the empty sink and leaving things wherever they landed. The mouse droppings soon came back as well.

That was the hardest part. It was not only the work itself. It was knowing that my effort meant nothing to anyone else. I could spend hours trying to improve things, and within days, sometimes less, it would all start sliding back again.

So I only did it a couple of times. I was so disappointed. I think, deep down, I wanted someone to notice. Not even in a dramatic way. Just a simple thank you, or even a bit of effort to keep it nice. But that never really happened.

My younger brother carried on that habit when we later lived together, using all the utensils and then piling them up in the sink without washing them. By that point, I think I had already had enough of living in other people's mess. I was so relieved when I eventually moved out on my own.

I know now that it was never just about the mess. It was about feeling invisible. No matter how much effort I put in, it was not noticed, not appreciated, and never enough to make a lasting difference. That feeling stayed with me for a long time in that house. I could work hard, clean, help, try to make things better, and still feel as though none of it mattered.

So when I finally moved out on my own, it was not just about having a different place to live. It was about having space that belonged to me. A place where mess did not build up unless I allowed it to. A place where my efforts were not constantly undone by someone else's carelessness.

It might sound small, but it meant everything. For the first time, I could close the door and know that the space inside was mine. I could clean something and it would stay clean. I could breathe without feeling surrounded by clutter, dirt, and other people's neglect.

For years, I had been moved from room to room, pushed into corners, made to sleep in spaces that never really felt like mine, and expected to cope with whatever was left around me. The loft, the sofa, the dirty collars, the crowded house, the cats, the mess, the kitchen that never stayed clean; all of it taught me that I did not really have a place.

But I wanted one. I think I had always wanted one. Not just a bedroom or a tidy kitchen, but somewhere I could feel settled and safe. Somewhere I did not have to hide the state of my clothes, or sleep in my uniform to keep warm, or clean for hours just to feel normal for a day.

That is what those years did to me. They made me grateful for things other people might not even think about. A clean sink. A warm bed. A closed door. A quiet room. A place where I could finally feel like I belonged.

Chapter 7
Art, Haircuts & Tattoos

"It is hard to grow into yourself when someone else keeps deciding who you are supposed to be."

In Year Nine, I was asked to choose what I wanted to study for my GCSEs. I did not know exactly what I wanted to do with my life at that age. Most children do not. But I knew I loved History and English, so I put those down on my list. They were subjects that felt interesting to me, subjects where I felt I could think for myself and enjoy what I was learning.

For once, it felt like I had made a choice that belonged to me. It was not some huge life decision, but it mattered. At that age, even a small choice can feel important because it is part of learning who you are. I went through Year Ten with the subjects I had picked, and I was doing fine. I was managing. There was no real problem until my mother decided there was one.

When I was nearly at the end of Year Ten, my mother told me I needed to do Art because, according to her, I was not good at anything else. That hurt more than I probably let on at the time. It was not just about being told to take another subject. It was being told that the things I had chosen were wrong, and that I was not capable enough to make decisions for myself.

I did not want to do Art, but as with so many things in my childhood, what I wanted did not really matter. She took me into school and spoke to the teachers, even though I had almost finished Year Ten by then. She told them I had made a mistake when choosing my subjects and persuaded them to let me take GCSE Art instead.

I remember feeling embarrassed and powerless. It was my education, but I was not the person being listened to. I was there, but somehow not really included in the decision.

I do not know how she managed it, but getting what she wanted was something she was always very good at. The school allowed me to take the subject, but because I was starting so late, I only had one year to do what everyone else had two years to complete.

That is when she really took over. She actually did most of the work when I was at home, and I only did some of it in the classroom. But even then, the ideas were not mine. The colours, the designs, the direction of the work, all of it came from her. Nothing really came from my own mind.

That is a strange thing to admit because, on paper, it was my GCSE. It had my name on it. But it never truly felt like my work. It felt like I was simply the person carrying out something she had decided. Even when I was holding the pencil or paintbrush, I did not feel like the one in control.

She was living through me, and she continued doing that throughout my education. I had very little say in what I studied or what direction my life was taking. It felt as though she had already written a version of me in her head, and I was expected to become that person whether I wanted to or not.

It was exhausting. Not in a loud or dramatic way all the time, but in a quiet, constant way. I did not feel encouraged. I felt managed. I did not feel guided. I felt controlled. I was growing up, but instead of discovering who I was, I was being pushed into someone else's idea of who I should be.

When it came to college, the same thing happened again. My mother chose the Art course for me. There was no proper conversation about what I wanted, no sitting down with me to talk through options, no encouragement to think about my own future. She simply decided, and that was that.

What made it harder was that she did not do the same thing with my brothers. They were allowed to make their own choices. My older brother chose to study Art on his own, and she did not try to force him into anything. My younger brother chose IT at college. They seemed to have the freedom to decide what suited them.

I noticed that difference. Of course I did. I might not have said much about it, but I felt it. I was the one being directed, shaped, and pushed. My life seemed to be the one she felt entitled to interfere with the most.

My mother became very excited about the shows my Art class put on. She would get dressed up, wearing make-up and nice clothes, as if she were going to present the work herself. From the outside, it probably looked like a proud mother coming to support her daughter.

But to me, it did not feel that simple. It felt as though she was enjoying the attention around something she had pushed me into. She looked like a normal mother, proud and involved, but I knew how much of that work had come from her ideas, her choices, and her need to be part of it.

There is something painful about watching someone take pride in a version of you they created, especially when they have ignored the real person underneath.

On the side, I chose a photography course. It was only a small extra course, but I enjoyed it very much. Photography felt different. It felt like something I had chosen for myself, something that did not come with the same pressure or sense of being watched.

I loved taking photographs, and I still do. There was something peaceful about it. A photograph allowed me to notice things in my own way. I could choose what to focus on, what to frame, what mattered in that moment. Maybe that is why I loved it so much. It gave me a little bit of control in a life where control was usually taken from me.

If I had been allowed to choose for myself at university, I probably would have chosen Photography. It is strange because my mother always had a camera in her hand, so you would think she might have understood that interest. But my interest only seemed to matter if it fitted with what she wanted for me.

But, of course, I was not really given a choice. I remember looking through the prospectus, trying to see what courses were available. That should have been an exciting thing, really. It should have been about imagining possibilities and thinking about what kind of life I might want.

Instead, she snatched the prospectus from me, went straight to the Art section, and said, "There is interior design or glass design for you to choose from."

That was it. My choice had been narrowed down before I had even had the chance to explore it properly. So the decision was made for me, as so many decisions had been. I was not asked who I wanted to become. I was told which version of myself I was allowed to be.

Even now, I sometimes wonder what path my life might have taken if I had been allowed to choose for myself. I wonder what might have happened if someone had simply asked me what I wanted and actually cared about the answer.

Photography gave me a glimpse of something that felt like mine. It brought me joy without pressure. It did not feel like a performance. It did not feel like something I had to do to please someone else. But like so many things, it was quietly pushed out of reach.

I did try to make the most of what I was given. I often did. That is what you do when you have very little say. You try to cope with the choices made for you and convince yourself it is fine. But deep down, it never really felt like my life. It felt like I was living inside a plan someone else had written, while my own wants sat quietly in the background, waiting to be noticed.

"Sometimes it is not just the hair being cut away. It is confidence, comfort, and the feeling that your body belongs to you."

At fourteen, I begged my mother for weeks to let me have my hair cut. I hated my hair at the time, and I was bullied a lot because of it. I had long, curly hair, and I did not know how to manage it properly. Nobody had taught me how to care for it, style it, or feel good about it.

Eventually, she agreed, but instead of taking me to a hairdresser, she told me to wash my hair and put it in a ponytail. Then, in her anger, she cut it at the top of the ponytail.

There was no gentleness in it. No thought about how it would look. No care for how I would feel afterwards. It was treated like a chore, or perhaps even a punishment, rather than something that mattered to me.

After that, my hair was a frizzy mess. Because I had not been taken to a hairdresser, there was no proper shape, no advice, no styling tips, nothing. I was already self-conscious, and now I felt even worse.

At that age, appearance can feel like everything. School can be cruel, and other children notice anything that makes you stand out. I already felt awkward enough, and my hair became one more thing to be embarrassed about.

For some reason, when I was sixteen, I begged her to cut it again. I do not know why I trusted her to do it better that time. Maybe I was still hoping she would listen. Maybe I was still hoping for the kind of mother who would care about how I felt.

This time, she cut it extremely short. I could feel how short it was becoming, and I started flinching. She asked why I was flinching, and I said, "It just feels really short." Her response was, "It's fine, stop fussing."

But it was not fine to me. I was the one who had to wear it. I was the one who had to go to school with it, face people, and feel exposed. But once again, my discomfort was treated as an inconvenience.

It was as short as my brothers' haircuts, because she cut their hair too. I honestly wanted the ground to swallow me up.

I felt humiliated. Not just because of the haircut, but because I had no control over it. My own appearance did not feel like mine. My hair, my clothes, my education, my choices; so much of it seemed to belong to her before it ever belonged to me.

When I started working at sixteen, I met my now best friend. She introduced me to hair straighteners and make-up, neither of which I had any experience with. It might sound like a small thing, but it was actually one of the best things for me at that time.

For the first time, I had someone showing me how to feel a little better about myself. Not in a vain way, but in a normal teenage way. I was learning things that many girls had probably learnt at home from their mothers, sisters, or friends. For me, it felt almost new and strange, as though I was catching up on parts of growing up that I had missed.

I have only recently, at the age of thirty-nine, stopped straightening my hair and started learning how to style it naturally. I have been to a few hairdressers who have given me advice, and now I actually love my natural hair. I get compliments on it all the time.

That still feels strange to me sometimes, because I spent so many years fighting against it, hiding it, changing it, and feeling ashamed of it. It has taken me a long time to realise that there was never anything wrong with my hair. I just had not been taught how to care for it, or for myself, in a kind way.

"Even when I tried to make a choice for myself, I still asked for permission."

At seventeen, nearly eighteen, my best friend and I decided we wanted either a tattoo or a belly button piercing. Most people that age might have just done it, or at least made the decision for themselves. But I still asked my mother.

Even at seventeen, I would not have dared to get something like that without her approval. That says a lot about the hold she still had over me. I was nearly an adult, but I still felt like I needed permission to do anything with my own body.

She told me she would rather I got a tattoo than a piercing, which I still find strange because a tattoo is permanent and a piercing can simply be taken out. But, of course, there was a condition. I could only get a tattoo that she had designed.

So even this was not really mine. Not fully. It was my skin, my body, and something I was choosing to do, but she still found a way to put herself into it.

Because I really wanted the tattoo, I agreed to let her design it. She drew a rose. I took the drawing to a tattoo artist, and because I was not quite eighteen, I had to lie about my age. Back then, they did not ask for proof, so he agreed to do it.

He told me he would not be able to make it look exactly like the drawing, but I did not see that as a problem. To me, that was normal. A tattoo artist would obviously need to adapt a drawing so it worked as a tattoo. I thought it would be fine.

But I was wrong.

When I got home and showed it to my mother, she was furious. Apparently, it looked nothing like the one she had drawn. I had expected maybe a comment, maybe some disappointment, but not that level of anger.

She did not speak to me for a month. That is a very awkward and painful thing when you live in the same house as someone. She would walk past me and completely blank me, as if I was not there. Although, to be fair, I did not see her much anyway because she barely got out of bed.

Still, being ignored like that by your own mother leaves a mark. It was not just silence. It was punishment. It was a way of making me feel that I had done something terrible, even though all I had done was get a tattoo she had agreed to, based on a design she had chosen.

That was often how it worked with her. Even when I followed the rules, the rules could change. Even when I tried to please her, I could still get it wrong. And when I got it wrong, the punishment was not always shouting. Sometimes it was being treated like I did not exist.

By that point in my life, I had already had so many choices taken from me that I barely knew how to make one without feeling guilty. My education had been decided for me. My appearance had been shaped without care. Even something as personal as a tattoo became about her feelings, her design, her approval.

I did not understand it fully then, but I can see it now. It was never really about Art, hair, or a tattoo. It was about control. It was about growing up with someone who could not let me become myself without trying to step in and claim part of it. And for a long time, I let her, because I did not know there was any other way to live.

Chapter 8
Tears For Attention

After being ignored for a month over the tattoo, I was already used to silence being used as punishment. But my mother had other ways of making us feel guilty too. Sometimes it was silence. Sometimes it was anger. And sometimes it was crying in a way that made us feel as though we were responsible for fixing her.

"It is a strange thing to be a child and feel responsible for your mother's unhappiness."

One thing my mother had always done was cry in her bedroom, which unfortunately was right next to the bathroom. At first, all three of us would go into her room to hug her. We were children, and when your mother cries, your first instinct is to comfort her. You do not stop to wonder whether it is too much for you to carry. You just want her to be all right.

My older brother was the first to stop going in. Then I stopped. Then my younger brother stopped too. I do not think any of us made a big decision about it. I think, over time, we just became tired. There are only so many times a child can be pulled into an adult's sadness before something inside them starts to shut down.

The problem was that when we stopped going into her room, she would come out onto the landing and cry there instead. If we needed the bathroom, we had no choice but to walk past her. There was no way around it.

At first, if she was only crying, we would give her a hug and then go to the bathroom. That became another strange routine in the house. You might be half-asleep, or just trying to brush your teeth, and there she would be, crying on the landing, waiting to be comforted.

It sounds odd to say it like that, but that is how it felt. Her sadness was placed in the middle of the house, where we could not avoid it.

Then it became worse. She started telling whichever one of us happened to walk past that we had ruined her life. She said she could have had a much better life if she had not had to look after the three of us. She could have gone travelling. She could have met a nice man. She could have done all these things, apparently, if we had not existed in the way.

I do not think any child should ever hear that from their mother. Children do not ask to be born. They do not choose the life their parents have. But when you are told often enough that you are the reason someone is unhappy, part of you begins to believe it.

To hear your own mother say those things is horrible. There is no softer way to put it. And the worst part is that after hearing it so many times, you do start to ignore it, or at least you try to.

But ignoring something is not the same as it not hurting. It still goes in. It still sits somewhere inside you. You might roll your eyes, walk away, or pretend you have heard it all before, but a child's heart still hears, "I would have been happier without you."

"Leaving should have felt like freedom, but she made it feel like abandonment."

When I turned eighteen, my best friend and I went to look at a house to rent because we both wanted to move out and live independently. It should have been exciting. Most young people want that feeling of having their own place, making their own rules, and starting to feel like an adult. I wanted that too.

At the time, I was paying my mother £200 a month from my supermarket job. I was not getting much for that money except a roof over my head. There was no real comfort in the house, no warmth, and no feeling of belonging. It felt more like I was there because I had to be, not because I was loved or wanted there.

Our evening meals were either very late at night or did not happen at all. When they did happen, they were nearly always the same: mince with potatoes and kidney beans. It was bland and repetitive, and there were nights when I went to bed still hungry.

That is where the cats came in handy, because they were always happy to share. It sounds strange, but sometimes I felt more looked after by them than by my own mother. They did not judge me. They did not make me feel guilty. They simply stayed close, and in that house, even that felt like something.

Once my friend and I had decided that the house we viewed was perfect for us, I went home and told my mother I was planning to move out. It did not go well. Her mood changed almost immediately.

She told me I could not move out because, without my rent money, she would not be able to afford heating or food. She said she would freeze or starve to death. She also said she would lose the house and become homeless.

Those words were not just guilt trips. They felt sharp and deliberate. She knew exactly where to press. She knew I already felt responsible for her feelings, and now she made me feel responsible for her survival too.

So I stayed. I felt overwhelmed by guilt and fear. I truly believed that if I left, something terrible would happen and it would be my fault. It did not matter that I was only eighteen and trying to start my own life. In that moment, all I could think about was what might happen to her if I chose myself.

My friend was not happy about it, and I understand why. From the outside, it must have looked simple. I had a chance to move out, so why did I not just go? But she did not understand how much of a hold my mother had over me.

My friend had grown up in a normal, loving household. She knew what it felt like to be supported. I did not. It is very hard to explain emotional manipulation to someone who has not lived under it. It makes even the most normal choices feel selfish. Moving out did not feel like growing up. It felt like abandoning my mother and leaving her to suffer.

That was the part people could not see. I was not just making decisions based on what I wanted. I was making them through years of guilt, fear, and being made to feel responsible for things that were never mine to carry.

One New Year, my younger brother and I went into town to celebrate. We were sitting with our friends in one of the pubs, doing something completely normal for people our age, when I looked out of the window and saw our mother standing there.

She was just watching us.

It was really unsettling. We had not invited her to join us, and I still do not know what she was doing there. My brother and I were both over eighteen. We did not need her to keep an eye on us. But there she was, outside the pub, watching from a distance as if she still had every right to place herself in the middle of our lives.

That moment stayed with me because it showed how little privacy or independence we really had. Even when we were out with friends, even when we were adults, even when the night should have belonged to us, she found a way to be there.

She never truly let go. Not in the way a parent is supposed to. She did not step back and let us become our own people. She watched, interfered, guilted, and reminded us in small and not-so-small ways that freedom would always come with a cost.

By then, I was old enough to know I wanted a life of my own, but I was still not free enough to take it without fear. That was the hardest part. I wanted independence, but I had been trained to feel guilty for wanting it. I wanted space, but I did not know how to claim it without feeling cruel.

And that is what emotional control does. It does not always lock the door. Sometimes it makes you believe you are wrong for wanting to open it.

"Being locked out of your own home makes you realise how little safety you really have."

Even when I tried to have something that felt normal, like going out with friends, my mother still found a way to make it difficult. I was at an age where I should have been gaining confidence, having fun, and feeling a little more independent. Instead, even my nights out came with fear attached to them.

I went out every weekend with my friends. I was only 17, but my best friend was great at persuading the bouncers that I was 18. She turned 18 four months before me, and so she wanted to go clubbing. She was actually great for giving me the confidence that I was so clearly lacking.

In many ways, she was good for me. She gave me confidence that I clearly did not have on my own. Around her, I felt a bit braver. I could laugh, get ready, go out, and feel like a normal young person for a while. Those nights gave me a small taste of freedom, even if I was still carrying everything from home with me.

The problem, again, was my mother. She knew perfectly well that I had gone out, but on more than one occasion, she locked the door so I could not get back into the house.

That is difficult to explain without it sounding unbelievable. It was not as though I had disappeared without telling anyone. She knew I was out. She knew I would need to come home. But still, there were nights when I stood outside my own house and could not get in.

The first time she locked the door, I just used my key to push her key out of the lock so I could then get in. But of course, when she realised that I could do that, she then started to lock the door and then half-turn the key so it couldn't be pushed out.

That is how I know it was done on purpose, no matter how much she later tried to claim it had been an accident. An accident does not keep changing its method. An accident does not adjust itself so the person outside still cannot get in.

I had bought a cheap car from my grandad's neighbour for £50, and luckily, that was parked outside the house. So when my mother had locked the door, I just sat in my car. Still freezing, but at least I was safe.

I could not sleep. I just sat there and waited until someone unlocked the house in the morning. I remember the cold more than anything. The kind of cold that gets into your hands, your legs, your back. But I also remember the feeling of sitting outside the home I lived in and knowing the person inside had chosen not to let me in.

What mother would deliberately lock her daughter out at night?

I still ask myself that sometimes. Not because I do not know the answer, but because it is one of those things that never becomes normal, no matter how many years pass. A mother is supposed to worry if her daughter is outside late at night. Mine created the danger and then acted as though it was nothing.

I couldn't drive yet, but I bought the car because my mother wanted me to. At this point, I had no interest in learning to drive, but as usual, I had no choice. I took lessons when I was 17, but failed the test. I failed the theory test, which I paid for, but my mother was so mad at me for failing it. You would think it was her money I had lost.

I already felt embarrassed about failing. I did not need anger on top of it. I needed reassurance, or at least a normal response. Instead, it became another thing I had done wrong.

I had no interest in passing the test and so put no effort into it. I paid for all the driving lessons myself, so it made no difference to her if I passed or not. I think she was only annoyed because then she couldn't go around telling people that her daughter had passed her driving test on the first attempt.

I think the fact I didn't pass on my 1st attempt made her believe that I had failed her rather than myself. I failed her because she couldn't tell the world I passed, my failure was somehow her failure but worse.

I think everything about her is making out to everyone else how brilliant and talented her kids are, just to make herself look good. If we achieved something, it became something she could tell other people. If we failed, it reflected badly on her, or at least that is how she made it feel.

That kind of pressure is exhausting because you stop being a person and start feeling like evidence. Evidence that she was clever. Evidence that she was a good mother. Evidence that her children were successful because of her. But behind closed doors, the reality was very different.

By that age, I was trying to become independent, but every step towards freedom came with guilt, punishment, or some kind of control. I wanted to go out with friends, but I might be locked out. I wanted to move out, but I was made to feel responsible for whether my mother could survive. I was pushed to learn to drive, but only because it suited the image she wanted.

There was always a cost.

I think that is what made those years so confusing. From the outside, it may have looked as though I was growing up. I had a job. I went out with friends. I had a car. I was taking driving lessons. But inside, I still felt trapped. I still felt watched. I still felt as though my choices were never fully mine.

For me, life was not just about tears, guilt, or being locked out. It was about the way my mother made even ordinary parts of growing up feel unsafe. Moving out, going out, earning money, learning to drive, wanting space; all of it should have been normal. But with her, normal things became complicated. They became emotional traps.

Honestly, for a long time, I did not know how to step out of them. I only knew how to feel guilty, keep quiet, and try not to make things worse.

Chapter 9
University and My Mother's Interference

After years of being made to feel guilty for wanting ordinary things, university should have felt like freedom. It should have been my chance to breathe, to make friends, to make mistakes, to find out who I was without my mother standing over every choice. In some ways, I did get small pieces of that. I had moments where I laughed, dressed up, worked, made friends, and felt almost like other people my age.

But freedom is not easy when you have never really been taught how to have it. Even when I was away from home, my mother's voice was still there. It was in the way I doubted myself, the way I needed approval, the way I struggled to trust my own choices. I had left the house, but I had not yet escaped the hold she had over me.

"Sometimes freedom arrives quietly, in a new place, with new people, and one small moment where you finally feel like yourself."

I went to university when I was nineteen. My mother had chosen a glass and ceramics course for me, so even though I had moved away, the course itself still did not feel like something that truly belonged to me. It was another path she had chosen, another decision that had been made before I had the chance to properly ask myself what I wanted.

At that age, I should have been excited about starting a new chapter. I should have been nervous in a normal way, the way most young people are when they leave home and step into something unfamiliar. But I carried so much more than normal nerves. I carried years of being criticised, watched, corrected, and made to feel unsure of myself.

I had struggled to make friends since I was about ten years old. That still makes me sad, because I had not always been like that. As a very young child, I was confident. I was chatty, bright, and not afraid to be seen. Somewhere along the way, that changed. My mother knocked so much of that confidence out of me that by the time I went to university, I was shy, quiet, and careful around people.

I wanted friends, but I did not always know how to be around people without feeling awkward. I worried about saying the wrong thing. I worried about being judged. I worried that people would see something in me that I could not hide. When you grow up feeling as though you are always doing something wrong, that feeling does not simply disappear because you move into student accommodation.

I did make a couple of lovely friends. One friend in particular I got on with very well. She made friends easily, much more easily than I did, and through her there ended up being a small group of us. That helped me more than I probably realised at the time. I did not have to push myself into every conversation because she had a way of bringing people together.

Being around her gave me a little confidence. Not a lot, not all at once, but enough to make me feel less alone. I could join in. I could laugh. I could be part of something without feeling completely out of place. For someone who had spent so much of her childhood feeling like she did not quite belong anywhere, that mattered.

I bought a lovely black dress for the Christmas party. It might sound like such a small thing, but to me it felt special. I wanted to look nice. I wanted to feel grown up, pretty, and normal. I wanted to be like the other girls who seemed to know how to dress, how to stand, how to enjoy themselves without second-guessing every little thing.

My friend and I had a great time at the party. I remember that feeling because it was rare for me. I was not being laughed at. I was not being corrected. I was not being told I looked wrong or had chosen badly.

I was simply there, wearing something I liked, spending time with people I liked, and feeling for once that maybe I could be happy in my own skin.

Then the Christmas holidays came, and I went back home. I worked through all my holidays from university. I did enjoy working, but if I am honest, I also liked having a reason to be out of the house. Work gave me structure. It gave me people to talk to. It gave me a place where I could be useful without everything becoming emotional or complicated.

Being at work was easier than being at home for too long. Even if I was tired, I still preferred it. At work, I knew what was expected of me. At home, I never really knew what version of my mother I was going to get. I could walk into the house and feel the atmosphere before anyone even spoke.

So I worked as much as I could. It gave me distance, even if only for a few hours at a time. Sometimes distance is the only way you can breathe.

On Christmas Day, when we were going to visit my grandparents, I decided to wear the black dress. I had felt good in it at the university party, and I wanted to feel that way again. I wanted to look nice for Christmas. I wanted to wear something that made me feel pretty.

I got dressed up and came downstairs. Then my mother laughed at me and asked why I was wearing that.

That was all it took. One laugh. One question. Suddenly, I was not a young woman wearing a dress she liked. I was a silly girl who had got it wrong. I felt exposed, embarrassed, and stupid, as though I had tried to be something I had no right to be.

I went back upstairs to my room and cried. I cried because I was hurt, but also because I was angry with myself for caring so much. I wished I could have just shrugged it off. I wished I could have kept the dress on and ignored her. But I could not. Her opinion still had too much power over me.

I changed into my usual jeans and a jumper. They felt safer. They did not make me stand out. They did not invite comments. They were ordinary enough that I could disappear back into myself.

When my mother saw me again, she acted surprised and asked why I had changed. I just frowned at her. I did not know how to answer without making things worse. How was I supposed to say, "Because you laughed at me"? How was I supposed to explain that her reaction had made me feel ashamed of myself?

I had learnt by then that explaining my feelings to her rarely helped. Most of the time, it only gave her another chance to twist things, deny things, or make me feel dramatic. So I said nothing. I swallowed it, like I had swallowed so many things before.

This type of behaviour is part of what made everything so confusing. It was not really my choice to change outfits. She had made me feel that what I was wearing was stupid and that I looked ridiculous. Then, when I changed, she acted shocked and told me I had looked really pretty in the dress.

That was the part that messed with my head. She could make me feel ashamed, then act as though she had no idea why I was upset. She could wound me with a comment, then behave as though I had misunderstood the whole thing. It made me question my own reactions.

Was I too sensitive? Had I taken it the wrong way? Was she joking? Was I the problem?

Those questions followed me for years. That is what happens when someone keeps hurting you and then denying the hurt. You stop trusting your own feelings. You start needing proof for pain that should have been obvious.

That kind of emotional back-and-forth really does affect a person's mind. One moment, you are being mocked. The next, you are being praised for the very thing you were made to feel ashamed of. It leaves you constantly questioning yourself: your choices, your appearance, your memory, and even whether your feelings are reasonable.

I could never fully relax around her. I could never feel safe in my own skin. Every little step towards confidence felt fragile, as though it could be undone in a second by one laugh, one look, or one comment. Most of the time, it was.

The black dress stayed in my memory because it was not really about the dress. It was about how quickly joy could turn into shame around her. It was about how a small moment of confidence could be taken from me before I had even had the chance to enjoy it.

I had not done anything wrong. I had simply tried to feel nice. Somehow, even that became something I had to recover from.

"Failure feels different when the choice that caused it was never really yours."

My mother also decided what I should make for my second-year project at university. She even sent me drawings of what she thought I should make. This was supposed to be my course, my work, and my responsibility, but somehow she still found a way to involve herself in it.

By then, I was so used to following what she wanted that I did exactly what she had asked. I wish I had questioned it more. I wish I had trusted the project brief, my tutors, or even my own instincts. But trusting myself was not something I had been taught to do.

I failed the course because what she had designed had very little to do with the actual task I had been given. It also had very little glass involved, which was obviously not ideal for a glass-blowing challenge. Looking at it now, it seems so clear. At the time, I was still trapped in that old pattern of doing what she said and dealing with the consequences afterwards.

The failure felt humiliating because it had my name on it. My tutors were not marking my mother's interference. They were marking my project. To them, it was my work, my decision, my mistake. That made it even harder to bear, because I had to stand there and take responsibility for something that had never fully come from me.

I was so embarrassed when I went in to speak to the tutors about what I had made. I remember that horrible feeling of knowing, deep down, that the work was wrong before anyone even said it. I could feel it in the room. I could feel that I had not met what was expected.

When they told me I had failed the course, I burst into tears after leaving the room. I felt ashamed and disappointed in myself. I felt stupid. I felt as though I had proved my mother right in all the ways she had made me feel incapable.

But the truth is, I was not incapable. I had been pulled away from the actual task. I had followed someone else's idea because I had been trained to believe that doing otherwise would be wrong.

I was then asked to make three glasses in blown glass so I could pass the course, and I did. That part matters because it showed I could do it when I was actually doing what the course required. I could pass. I could complete the work. I could manage.

That should have been a lesson in trusting myself, but it took me years to really understand it. At the time, I mostly felt relief that I had passed and shame that I had failed in the first place. I did not yet have the confidence to say, even to myself, that my mother's interference had caused damage.

University should have been where I began to build myself. It should have been a place where I learnt independence, not just in the practical sense, but emotionally too. I should have been learning to choose, to try, to fail safely, to grow, and to discover what I liked without fear.

Instead, I was still untangling myself from my mother. Even when she was not beside me, she was still there in the way I made decisions. She was there in the guilt I felt when I wanted something different. She was there in my hesitation, my self-doubt, and my fear of getting things wrong.

Still, university gave me small glimpses of something better. It gave me friends. It gave me nights where I laughed. It gave me that black dress before it became tangled in shame. It gave me moments where I felt almost separate from the version of myself she had tried to create.

Those moments mattered. They were not enough to free me completely, but they showed me that another version of life existed. A version where I could choose what to wear, who to spend time with, what to enjoy, and who I might become. I did not know how to reach that life properly yet, but for the first time, I could see little pieces of it.

That is why this time in my life feels so complicated. University was both freedom and not freedom. I was away from home, but still carrying home inside me. I was starting to live my own life, but still letting my mother's choices shape it. I was becoming an adult, but emotionally I was still that child trying not to upset her.

It would take much longer for me to understand that leaving home was not the same as being free. Sometimes the hardest part is not getting out of the house. It is learning how to get someone else's voice out of your head, especially when it has been louder than your own for most of your life.

Chapter 10
Cutting to Survive

University had given me small moments of freedom, but it had not taken away the fear of what was waiting for me afterwards. The closer I came to the end of my course, the more that fear grew. Other people seemed to be thinking about their next steps, their futures, where they might go and what they might do. I was thinking about going back to my mother's house.

That thought frightened me more than I knew how to explain.

"Sometimes pain becomes the only thing a person can control when everything else feels impossible."

It was in my last year of university that I started self-harming. I was cutting myself because the thought of moving back in with my mother terrified me. That is the truth of it.

I was sexually abused by my uncle as a child, and my family thinks my self-harming was because of that. What happened to me was traumatic, of course it was, but that was not the reason I started hurting myself. The fear of going back home was what pushed me there. The thought of returning to that house, to her moods, her control, her guilt, and that awful trapped feeling, became too much for me to manage.

I did not know how to say, "I cannot go back there." I did not know who would listen if I did. I had spent so many years being taught to cope, stay quiet, and get on with things that I did not know how to ask for help in a way that felt safe. So the pain turned inward. It became something I could control when everything else felt out of my hands.

I hid the cuts well. Glass blowing made that easier because I wore arm covers, so no one questioned why my arms were covered. The rest of the time, I wore jumpers. I became good at hiding things, but I suppose I had already been doing that for most of my life. I had hidden shame, fear, embarrassment, hunger, neglect, and sadness. Hiding the cuts became another part of that.

I had nowhere else to go when I left university. That was the part that made everything feel so hopeless. If there had been another option, maybe things would have felt different. But I could not see one. The closer I got to leaving, the more anxious I became. It was not ordinary worry. It felt like dread building inside me, day after day, until I needed some kind of release from it.

Self-harm became that release. I am not proud of it, but I understand why I did it now. At the time, it felt like the only escape I had. Not a healthy escape, not a safe one, but the only one I could reach.

I am sure the sexual abuse I suffered affected the way I dealt with things. It would be impossible for something like that not to leave damage. But in my eyes, my mother caused the deeper fear in my everyday life. She was the person I should have been able to go to. She was the person who should have protected me, believed me, and made me feel safe.

I did not tell her what her brother was doing to me because I did not trust how she would react. That is heartbreaking to admit. A child should feel able to tell her mother when something terrible is happening. I did not. I was afraid she would accuse me of lying or say I was attention-seeking, because that was how she often made me feel.

She thought so little of me, or at least that is how it felt. So I kept it to myself. I carried something no child should have to carry, partly because the one person who should have been safest did not feel safe at all.

I was also worried about her mental health. She had told my brothers and me that she had tried to take her own life when we were young, while she was still married to our dad. I could never really understand why she told us that, but it made me afraid of upsetting her.

That was another burden placed on us far too early. Once a child hears something like that, they start measuring their words. They become careful. They worry that telling the truth might break the parent, or make things worse.

So there were many things I did not tell her when they happened to me. I did not tell her about the bullies at school. I did not tell her about the abuse. I did not tell her how frightened or lonely I really felt. I learnt to keep my pain quiet because her feelings always seemed more dangerous than mine.

It makes me incredibly sad to think how different my life might have been if I had had a stable and loving mother. Not a perfect mother, because no one is perfect, but someone safe. Someone I could have gone to. Someone who would have held me, believed me, and helped me instead of making me feel afraid of being honest.

So much of my life might have been different if I had not had to carry everything alone.

"Silence can be just as cruel as shouting when it is used to punish."

My friend and I went on holiday to Turkey for the third time, and while we were drunk, we decided to get tattoos that said Marmaris. I thought it was funny at the time. It was silly and impulsive, but it also felt like something normal young people might do on holiday.

There was something light-hearted about it, at least for a little while. A holiday, a friend, a ridiculous tattoo, a moment that was not meant to be deep or painful. It was just supposed to be a funny memory.

When we got home, my mother was lying in bed as usual, and she called me into her room. She grabbed my left arm and tried to pull up my sleeve, apparently to see my tan. I pulled away because that was the arm with the cuts on it.

That moment frightened me. I did not want her to see. I did not want questions, anger, disgust, or whatever reaction she might have had. I had worked so hard to hide it, and suddenly there was this real risk that she might find out.

It is strange, really, because part of me must have wanted someone to notice how much I was struggling. But not like that. Not her. Not in a way that would make me feel exposed and unsafe.

So she grabbed my other arm instead and pulled up that sleeve. Unfortunately, that was the arm with my new tattoo on it. She was furious.

Even then, I would still rather she saw the tattoo than the self-harm cuts and scars. That probably says a lot. I was more prepared for her anger over a tattoo than for her seeing the truth of how badly I was coping. A tattoo could be explained. A tattoo could be laughed off, argued about, or dismissed as a stupid mistake. The cuts would have shown something much deeper, and I did not trust her with that part of me.

What followed was another month of her not talking to me. She ignored me again, just as she had done before. Living in the same house as someone who refuses to speak to you is awful. It makes the whole house feel colder. You become aware of every movement, every doorway, every time you might pass each other.

It was not just that she was upset. It was punishment. She wanted me to feel her silence. She wanted me to know I had done something wrong and that I would be made to sit in it until she decided otherwise.

The silence only ended when my younger brother reminded her that she needed my rent money. That was what brought it to an end. Not concern. Not love. Not a real conversation. Money.

That hurt, although I do not think I let myself feel it properly at the time. I had become used to being useful in certain ways. My feelings did not matter much, but my rent did. My presence could be ignored, but my money could not.

By then, self-harm had become my secret way of surviving what I could not say out loud. I was frightened of going home, frightened of being trapped again, frightened of needing help from someone who had never made help feel safe. I was carrying trauma, shame, fear, and silence, all hidden under sleeves and jumpers.

From the outside, I probably looked like I was managing. I went to university. I went on holiday. I worked. I came home. I paid rent. But inside, I was falling apart in ways no one really saw.

That is one of the hardest parts to explain. People can look fine while they are barely coping. They can laugh on holiday, get a tattoo, go to work, sit in class, and still be breaking inside. I was not hurting myself because I wanted attention. I was doing it because I did not know how else to survive the fear, the guilt, and the thought of going back to a life that made me feel trapped.

I wish someone had seen through the surface. I wish someone had asked the right questions and stayed long enough to hear the real answers. More than anything, I wish I had felt safe enough to speak before the pain became something I turned on myself.

Chapter 11
Moving Back in With My Mother

After university, I had to return to the place I had been so frightened of going back to. I was no longer a child, but stepping back into that house made me feel as though very little had changed. I had more freedom in some ways because I was working and earning my own money, but emotionally, I was still living under my mother's control.

"Sometimes you can have a job, pay rent, and still feel trapped in the place you are meant to call home."

After I left university, I moved back in with my mother and into my old bedroom, as that room was free because my older brother was still away studying at university. In some ways, having my old bedroom back should have felt like a relief, especially after the loft, the sofa, and all the years of feeling pushed from one space to another.

But it did not really feel like coming home. It felt more like returning to a place I already knew was not good for me, because I had nowhere else to go.

I started working full-time at a supermarket. At the time, I was paying my mother £200 a month in rent. One summer, when a friend and I, along with one or two others, decided to take two trips to Turkey a couple of months apart, my mother decided that if I could afford to do that, then I could afford to pay more rent. So she put it up to £300 a month.

There was no proper conversation about it. It was just decided. I had worked for that money, saved for those holidays, and tried to have something enjoyable in my life. But instead of being happy that I was doing something for myself, she turned it into a reason to take more from me.

I did not complain. I just paid it. That was what I had learnt to do. Keep quiet, avoid the argument, and get on with it.

I know for a fact that my older brother never paid anything because he did not have a job until after university, and my younger brother was paying £200. I was paying more, but I was not getting much for it except a roof over my head in a filthy, mouse-infested house. Still, it felt better than being on the streets, so I accepted it.

That is the thing when you do not feel you have many options. You accept things that are unfair because the alternative feels even more frightening.

I bought myself a small TV for my bedroom, and honestly, it was one of the best things I could have done. I practically lived in that room, and I did not mind. It was peaceful and clean, which made it feel completely different from the rest of the house.

My bedroom became my little escape. It was the one place where I had some control. I could shut the door, keep it tidy, watch television, and feel separate from everything downstairs. The cats liked being in there too, so I usually had company. Their presence made the room feel warmer and less lonely.

It was not a perfect kind of independence, but it was the closest thing I had.

My best friend and I went on nights out a couple of times a week, and we used my bedroom as the place to get ready and have drinks before going out. My room was clean, comfortable, and honestly, if anything spilt, it was easier to sort out there than anywhere else in the house.

Because I went out a couple of times a week, my mother called me an alcoholic. That was not true. I was young, working full-time, and trying to have some kind of social life. But with her, normal behaviour could easily be turned into something shameful if it suited the story she wanted to tell.

The strange thing was that my bedroom was still the cleanest room in the whole house. It was so clean, in fact, that we used it for family birthdays with the four of us. That says a lot about the state of the rest of the house. My room was not just where I slept. It was the one space that felt cared for, because I was the one caring for it.

"The truth came out because my privacy was taken, but somehow that invasion became the thing that freed me."

I was still self-harming, and in fact, I continued doing so for ten years until I finally got the help I needed. At that time, I was still hiding it from everyone as best I could. I hid the things connected to it in my room, and because my bed was high off the ground, they could not easily be seen from floor level.

It is painful to think about how normal hiding had become for me. I hid my feelings, my fear, my memories, my shame, and now I was hiding the evidence of how badly I was struggling. From the outside, I was working, going out, paying rent, and getting on with life. Inside, I was still in survival mode.

It was only when my best friend saw my cuts during a night out that I finally sought help from the doctors. I think part of me must have known I needed help, but it took someone else seeing it for me to take that step.

After that, I received a letter from the doctor with the doctor's stamp on the envelope. My mother saw it because she was downstairs when it came through the letterbox. She asked my younger brother to bring it up to me, so I took it from him and closed the door.

Even then, I wanted privacy. I wanted one thing that belonged to me. One appointment. One small attempt at getting help without it becoming something for my mother to control.

I opened the letter and saw that it was an appointment to see a counsellor. I did not think any more of it. I put the letter to one side, got ready for work, and left the house.

I had no idea that while I was gone, my mother would go into my bedroom looking for that letter. She found it, then searched my room. In doing so, she found the things I had been using to self-harm, along with a letter I had written to a friend, who had given it back to me after reading it.

That letter held things I had not said out loud. Things I had been too frightened, ashamed, or confused to speak about properly. It was private. It was mine. But in that house, privacy never seemed to mean much if my mother wanted access to something.

In that letter, I had mentioned my uncle and the sexual abuse. I had written about self-harming and about wanting to see my dad since I was eighteen years old. Those were huge things to have sitting in a letter, and my mother found them all.

Sometimes I wish my friend had never handed the letter back to me. If she had kept it, my mother would not have found it. My private pain would not have been exposed in that way.

But the more I think about it, the more I am glad it happened. That sounds strange, because the way it happened was awful. But if my mother had not found that letter, she would not have thrown me out. If she had not thrown me out, I do not think I would have contacted my dad.

He would have died without me seeing him again. I truly believe that. As long as my mother was still in my life in that way, I do not think I would ever have found the courage to reach out to him. Her hold over me was too strong.

So as painful and violating as that moment was, it also became the beginning of something else. It was not freedom in a neat or gentle way. It was messy, frightening, and cruel. But it opened a door I might never have opened on my own.

Chapter 12

nselling and Being Thrown Out

mother found the letter, the blades, and the truth I had been
nard to hide, something shifted. Not in a gentle way. Not in
felt safe. But the things I had kept buried were now out in
and although that terrified me, it also began to loosen the
nad over me.

ng, I had protected her from the truth. I had hidden my
elf-harm, my anger, and even my need to see my dad. Once
ngs were discovered, I could no longer pretend everything

rst started seeing a counsellor, I did not really open up about
er. I made it seem as though my self-harming was because
cle's abuse. That abuse was real, and it had hurt me deeply,
s not the whole truth. It was not the main reason I was
yself.

living with my mother then, and she clearly still had a strong
me. Even in counselling, where I was supposed to be able
freely, I still protected her in a way. I still avoided naming
uth. I think part of me was frightened of what would happen
ed out loud that the thought of living with my own mother
made me feel so trapped and desperate.

strange kind of loyalty that can grow out of fear. It does
sense from the outside, but when you are living inside it, it
ssible to break.

e time I was seeing this counsellor, my mother threw me
wful as that was, it also meant I could finally speak more
Once I was no longer living under her roof, I felt freer to

"A diary should be a safe place. Mine became another place she entered without permission."

My mother had suggested that I write a diary, which was not something I had really considered before. At the time, I thought it sounded like a good idea. I was going through so much. I felt overwhelmed, confused, angry, frightened, and constantly on edge. The idea of having somewhere private to put my thoughts felt comforting.

So I bought a simple notebook and started writing. For a while, it felt like a small sanctuary. It was a place where I could be honest without worrying about someone interrupting me, dismissing me, or telling me I was wrong. I could write the things I did not feel safe enough to say out loud.

Or at least, I thought I could.

I had no idea that while I was out working, my mother was going into my room and reading my diary. It did not once occur to me that I would need to hide it. Not because I believed she respected boundaries, but because I did not think anyone could be that cruel, especially not the person who had encouraged me to write it in the first place.

That is what made it feel so calculated. She had suggested the diary, watched me create that private space, then entered it when I was not there. It was not just nosiness. It felt like a trap I had unknowingly walked into.

It did not help that I was often angry with her, so of course I wrote things about her in it. Honest things. Hurt things. Things I did not feel safe enough to say to her face. That diary became the only place where I could tell the truth without being punished for it.

Then even that was taken from me.

Knowing now that she was reading it makes my skin crawl. It was more than a betrayal. It was manipulative, calculated, and deeply violating. She did not just read words on a page. She entered the one place where I thought my thoughts were safe.

Afterwards, she would bring up things I had written, although never directly. She would make comments that lined up too perfectly with what I had confided in those pages. She never had to admit she had read it. I knew.

I felt exposed and humiliated. It made me stop writing altogether. What was the point in expressing myself if even my most private thoughts were not safe?

That kind of invasion changes something in you. It teaches you that there is nowhere to put your feelings. Not in your room, not in a letter, not in a diary, not even inside yourself without wondering if someone will find a way to use it against you.

That diary had been my attempt to process years of confusion and hurt. Like so many other things in my life, she twisted it into another tool to control me.

Moving back in with my mother was never really about moving back into a house. It was about returning to an environment where I was watched, judged, searched, and used. I had a job and paid rent, but I was still not treated like a person with privacy or dignity. My bedroom was supposed to be my safe place, yet even that was not safe from her.

Still, the painful truth is that this chapter of my life became a turning point. Being searched, exposed, and thrown out was awful. It should not have happened that way. But it forced something open. It broke the hold just enough for me to reach towards my dad, the person I had wanted to see for years but had been too frightened to contact.

I wish it had happened differently.
calmly, with support and dignity. I
help without being violated first. But
clean escape. It gave me a painful or

Even so, that painful escape led me
as much as I hate what happened, p
that the truth finally came out.

Cou

After my
trying so
a way tha
the open,
hold she

For so lo
pain, my
those thi
was fine.

When I fi
my moth
of my un
but it wa
cutting m

I was still
hold over
to speak
the full tr
if I admit
was what

There is
not make
feels imp

During th
out. As a
honestly.

talk about wanting to see my dad. That had been sitting inside me for years, but I had been too frightened to do anything about it while she still had so much control over my life.

The GP also put me on antidepressants, which helped to stabilise my mood. I had become an angry person by then, but not in a way that hurt other people. Most of that anger was turned inward. I carried it inside myself, along with shame, fear, and sadness. I did not know how to let it out safely, so it stayed in me and became part of how I survived.

"One friend request was enough to expose how much control she still expected to have."

Not long after my mother found out about my uncle abusing me and about my self-harming, she threw me out. Before that happened, she came into my room one day shouting at me to give her my Facebook password. I cannot remember exactly why she wanted it, but I remember the feeling of being cornered.

I just wanted her to leave me alone. When someone is shouting and you are already emotionally exhausted, sometimes you give in simply to make it stop.

To get her away from me, I gave her the password. After that, I did not think much more about it. I actually forgot she had it.

Some time later, my cousin on my dad's side sent me a friend request, and I accepted it. Within about five minutes, I heard my mother crying to my older brother in his room, which was next to mine.

That is how quickly she saw it. That is how closely she must have been watching. It was not just about Facebook. It was about access. It was about keeping an eye on who I spoke to, especially if they were connected to my dad.

She was already in my brother's room, complaining about something, and must have seen that I had accepted the request. My brother had a computer, so I assume Facebook was open. The next minute, she came storming into my bedroom and started shouting at me.

She was furious that I had accepted the request. Her biggest concern seemed to be that my dad would now find out everything about her family.

That reaction told me so much. It was not about me reconnecting with family. It was not about whether I was okay, or whether I needed support, or why I might want contact with my dad's side. It was about what might be exposed. It was about what she might lose control of.

My other uncle had told me that our mother once said she would disown any of us if we saw our father. In that moment, it felt as though she meant it. She gave me a month to find somewhere else to live because she said she did not want anything to do with me anymore.

Hearing that from your own mother is hard to describe. Even when the relationship has been painful for years, some part of you still hopes there is a line she will not cross. Being told to leave made it clear that, to her, my need to reconnect with my dad was a betrayal.

She did not see it as me needing family. She saw it as me choosing against her.

"She did not just throw me out. She kept pieces of my life behind."

It had not even been a week when I went out with friends to celebrate the New Year. I stayed that night at a friend's house, and the next day I received a text from my younger brother. He told me our mother was going to throw all my things out onto the street if I did not come and get them.

I remember the panic of that moment. It was not just about belongings. It was the feeling that my whole life could be bagged up, thrown out, and treated as though it meant nothing.

I started to panic because I did not have a vehicle to put everything in. Thankfully, my younger brother said he would collect my things and bring them to me. My friend's parents were also kind enough to let me store my belongings in their caravan and stay with them until I found a flat I could afford.

That kindness meant more than I can say. At a time when my own mother was pushing me out, other people stepped in and gave me somewhere to stand. They did not make a performance of it. They simply helped. That kind of practical kindness can feel enormous when you have spent years feeling like a burden.

My younger brother brought my things in bin bags, with most of my belongings stuffed inside. Later, I found out that my mother had kept the things she knew were most important to me.

The only important thing she seemed to let go of was one photograph my grandad had printed for me and that had been on my wall. It was a photograph of me, and I found it screwed up at the bottom of one of the bags.

Seeing it like that hurt. A photograph is such a small thing, but it was mine. It was part of my life, part of how I remembered myself. Finding it crumpled at the bottom of a bag felt careless and cruel, as though even the image of me had been treated like rubbish.

She kept my photographs and my memory box because, apparently, I did not deserve them. I had nine albums full of my life, from when I started college, through holidays with my friends, to my university days. Those albums held years of memories. They were not valuable in a money sense, but they were valuable to me.

Photographs matter when your memories have already been made difficult to trust. They give you proof that you were there, that you lived those moments, that there were parts of your life beyond the pain. To have them kept from me felt like another punishment.

I do not know if those albums are still safe or if she has destroyed them. I will not see them again until she passes away, if they still exist at all. That is a very strange kind of grief, mourning things that may still be sitting somewhere, just out of reach.

The bags were stored in the caravan, and I was so grateful for that. My brother also told me he would come with me, which was amazing because I had already looked at flats, and the cheapest one I could find was £500 a month, not including bills. On my supermarket salary, there was no way I could afford that by myself.

Having him come with me made the impossible feel slightly more possible. I was frightened, but I was not completely alone. After years of feeling trapped, I was suddenly being pushed out into the world with very little warning, and I had to work out how to survive outside the only home I had known, even if that home had never really felt safe.

I got the flat. It was a nice two-bedroom, and although everything felt uncertain, it was still a beginning. Not the beginning I would have chosen, and not the gentle start I probably needed, but a beginning all the same.

Being thrown out was painful. It was frightening, humiliating, and cruel. But it also forced a separation that I do not think I could have created on my own at that point. My mother had spent years making me feel guilty for wanting anything outside of her control. Suddenly, I had no choice but to live outside of it.

I lost things in that process. I lost photographs, memories, the last pieces of my childhood that had been kept in boxes and albums. I lost any remaining illusion that my mother would protect the parts of me that mattered.

But I also gained something, even if I could not fully see it yet. I gained distance. I gained the smallest bit of space to think without her always being there. I gained the possibility of speaking honestly in counselling. Most importantly, I gained the chance to reach for my dad again.

At the time, it felt like everything was falling apart. In some ways, it was. But sometimes the thing that breaks your life open is also the thing that lets the light in.

Chapter 13
A Letter Full of Hurt, Not Love

After being thrown out, getting the flat, and finally having some distance from my mother, I think part of me still hoped there might be a softer ending between us. Not a perfect one. Not even a proper apology. Just something that showed she still saw me as her daughter. Two months later, a letter arrived, and for a brief moment, I let myself believe it might be kind.

"Some letters are not written to heal. Some are written to wound."

It was two months after my mother threw me out that a letter arrived for my brother and me. Our older brother brought them to us, one each, both in separate envelopes. He would not have known what was written inside them.

Mine had a lovely little charm attached to the envelope, and, stupidly, that made me think it might be a nice letter. I think some part of me still wanted to believe that. Even after everything, I still wanted there to be love there somewhere. I wanted to open it and find regret, care, or even just a few words that sounded like a mother missing her daughter.

I was wrong.

My letter was thirty-five pages long. My brother's was only about five pages. Mine was awful. It was full of cruelty, blame, and words no mother should ever write to her child. She wrote things like, "so why would I write to a child now dead to me," and accused me of "murdering" her precious child so I could be loved by a father she claimed had always had the chance to collect us. She also wrote, "keep drinking, keep cutting, keep abusing."

I still struggle to understand how a mother could write those words knowing her daughter had been self-harming. She knew I was in pain, and instead of offering care, she used that pain against me. The letter did not feel like something written by a mother who was hurt and wanted to mend things. It felt like something written to punish me.

Thirty-five pages is a lot of space to use against someone. Page after page, it felt as though she was trying to rewrite everything, to make herself the victim and me the cruel one. I had been thrown out, exposed, hurt, and frightened, yet somehow I was the one being blamed.

After reading the letter, I was in floods of tears. I was so hurt and angry that I harmed myself, and I still have a scar from that night. I do not say that for sympathy. I say it because that is how deeply those words affected me. They did not just upset me. They broke something open.

What made it even harder was knowing that the letter she wrote to my brother was completely different. His was full of love. She wrote about what a lovely man he had grown into and how proud she was of him. Mine was full of blame and rejection.

That difference hurt in a way I cannot properly describe. It was not only the cruelty of my own letter. It was the comparison. It showed me, in writing, how differently she saw us. One child was praised. I was attacked. One child was loved. I was made to feel dead to her.

I have only been able to read that letter all the way through once. It is too distressing, especially because it came from my own mother. There are some words you can move past, and there are others that stay lodged somewhere inside you. That letter stayed.

She called me an abuser in it, which felt like such a cruel reversal of the truth. I had spent years feeling controlled, frightened, guilty, and not good enough, yet somehow she made herself the victim and me the person who had harmed her.

That was how it often worked with her. Nothing was ever really her fault. Responsibility always seemed to move away from her and land on someone else.

This is how she has always been. She does not take responsibility for her actions. She blamed my dad for the way her marriage turned out. She blamed her hard-working parents for her childhood. She blamed me and my brothers for the life she believed she had missed out on.

She told us more than once that if it had not been for us, she could have met a lovely man, moved abroad, and had a great life. Hearing that as a child is one thing. Reading that same kind of blame as an adult, written out across pages, is another. It confirmed what I had felt for years: that she saw us not as children who needed love, but as reasons her life had not become what she wanted.

That letter should have been a bridge. It should have been a chance to speak with care, even if things were difficult. Instead, it became another wound, one made worse because I had briefly hoped it might contain love.

"Even when I finally tried to tell the truth, I was asked to protect everyone but myself."

I was really annoyed with myself because I had forgotten that I had given my mother my Facebook password. That meant she could see everything I was saying to my cousins, as I was friends with two of them at the time.

It made me feel foolish, but more than that, it made me feel watched all over again. I had moved out. I was no longer living under her roof. Yet somehow, she still had access to part of my private life. She could still see what I was saying, who I was speaking to, and what truths were beginning to come out.

One of the conversations was about going to the police to report my uncle. Because she could see my messages, my mother found out. She then turned up at our flat and just walked in.

She came to my room and said, "Can I have a word?" Then she got my brother as well. She was livid. She started talking about how she knew I was going to the police about my uncle.

It did not feel like concern. It did not feel like a mother wanting to support her daughter through something terrible. It felt like panic, anger, and control. She was not asking how I was. She was not asking what I needed. She was reacting to what my truth might do to other people.

My younger brother did not know this had happened to me, so he was in tears. My mother was crying too, and so was I. It was a horrible, overwhelming moment.

She told me I could not report it because my grandparents would never cope with the news, especially because it had happened in their house, where my uncle lived. She said it would destroy them.

Once again, the focus shifted away from me. I was the one who had been hurt, but somehow I was being asked to think about everyone else first. My grandparents' feelings. My mother's panic. The family's reaction. The damage it might cause outside of me.

No one seemed to stop and say, "What about what it did to you?"

So I did not report it then. I stayed quiet again, even though I should never have been made to feel responsible for protecting other people from the truth.

My cousins, however, were the ones who persuaded me to contact my dad. They told me he would be over the moon to hear from me. I wanted to believe that, but I was nervous. After so many years of being told different things, it was hard to know what was real. I did not know if he wanted to hear from me. I did not know if he would be angry, hurt, or distant.

I spoke to my counsellor about it because I did not even know how to begin the letter. I was not sure whether to write "Dear Dad" or use his name. My counsellor said to write "Dad" because he might be hurt if I used his name. So I did.

That tiny decision felt enormous. Writing "Dad" was not just a greeting. It was me reaching through years of silence, fear, and confusion. It was me allowing myself to call him what he had always been, even though I had been made to feel guilty for it as a child.

Apparently, when my dad received my letter, he cried because he was so happy.

I cannot think about that without feeling emotional. For years, I had believed all sorts of things about him, or at least had been made to doubt him. Yet there he was, crying because his daughter had finally reached out. He had not forgotten me. He had not stopped caring. He had been waiting.

"For the first time in years, love did not feel like something I had to earn."

After I got back in contact with my dad, my life began to change in ways I could not have imagined. Two years later, I moved across the road from him and to a different county from my mother. It was the best thing I have ever done.

When I first started seeing him again, he would drive down to pick me up and then take me home after our visits. He lived an hour and a half away, so that was not a small thing. It took time, effort, and care. He did it anyway.

That meant so much to me. I was not used to someone making that kind of effort just because they wanted to see me. I was not used to feeling chosen in such a steady, quiet way.

I did have a car by then, but I was not a confident driver, so it took a while before I drove myself to him. He never made me feel bad about that. He simply helped.

I did not tell my dad about my self-harming, but I did tell my cousin. I assume she told her mother, who then told my dad. Part of me felt frightened about him knowing, but another part of me was probably relieved. It is exhausting to keep pain hidden all the time.

The difference was that with my dad, knowing something painful about me did not turn into punishment. It did not become a weapon. It did not make me feel smaller.

My dad did know about my uncle, although I cannot remember whether I told him or whether my auntie did. I spoke to him about some of the things my mother had done, and he was surprised that she had been that bad.

He apologised to me as if it was his fault. That stayed with me because it showed the kind of person he was. He was not defensive. He did not make it about himself. He was sorry that I had suffered, even though he had not been the one who caused it.

He told me she had been bad when he was married to her, but it sounded as though she had got worse. I think that must have been painful for him too, knowing he had not been able to protect us from what happened after the visits stopped.

Moving closer to my dad also led me to meet my now husband, and I am so happy. I wish more than anything that my dad were still here and could have met him. They would have got on so well. That thought hurts, because after everything it took to find my way back to my dad, I wanted more time.

I did get six years with him, and I am grateful for every one of them. In those six years, I got to know what a wonderful man he was. Not the version of him I had been told about as a child, but the real him. Kind, gentle, thoughtful, and loving in ways that were simple but deeply meaningful.

He made me beautiful items as gifts, things I will treasure for the rest of my life. Those gifts mattered because they were made with care. They were not about control or guilt. They were not given with conditions. They were just love, made into something I could hold.

He used to make lovely cakes, and he would leave me a slice in an ice cream box with a lid on it outside my front door for when I got home from work in the morning, because I worked nights.

The first time he did it, I cried. It was such a small gesture, but to me it felt enormous. Someone had thought of me. Someone had made something and left it there because they knew I would be tired after work. Someone had cared about me without making me feel guilty for needing care.

I had never felt loved like that before. Not in such a calm, ordinary, gentle way. That was what made it so powerful. It was not dramatic. It was not performative. It was just my dad, leaving cake at my door because he loved me.

That kind of love changed something in me. It showed me that love did not have to hurt. It did not have to come with fear, silence, guilt, or conditions. Love could be quiet. Love could be practical. Love could be a lift home, a handmade gift, a slice of cake waiting outside the door.

After so many years of being made to feel difficult, unwanted, or responsible for everyone else's pain, my dad gave me something I had needed for a very long time. He gave me the feeling of being wanted.

That letter from my mother was full of hurt, but reaching out to my dad brought me back to something real. It did not erase the pain, and it did not give back the years we had lost. Nothing could do that. But it gave me the chance to know him, love him, and be loved by him while there was still time.

For that, I will always be grateful.

Chapter 14
Reporting The Sexual Abuse

After finding my way back to my dad, I had started to feel something I had not felt for years: a little bit of distance from my mother's control. Not complete freedom, but enough to breathe. Enough to begin building a life that did not revolve around her moods, her rules, or her version of the truth.

Then, years later, she found a way to place herself back into one of the most painful parts of my life.

"The truth should have been mine to tell, but even that was taken out of my hands."

I received a phone call from the police. An officer told me that my mother had been to see them to make a complaint about my uncle. Hearing that was confusing straight away, because this was something my mother had once persuaded me not to report.

I later found out that she had not even gone to the police because of me at first. She had gone there to complain about my uncle's soon-to-be wife because she had the same first name as my mother, which meant they would end up with the same name.

That still feels unbelievable to me. Out of everything she could have been concerned about, that was what took her to the police. Not what had happened to me. Not the pain I had carried. Not justice. A name.

When the police told her there was nothing they could do about that, she then decided to tell them that I had been sexually abused by him when I was younger.

That was my story. My trauma. My choice to speak or not speak should have belonged to me. Yet somehow, even that became something she used when it suited her. She had once told me not to report it because it would destroy my grandparents. Now, when it served her own purpose, she told the police herself.

I cannot explain how angry that made me. Not because the truth came out, but because of the way it came out. Once again, she had taken something deeply personal from me and made herself the person in control of it.

"Justice mattered, but so did the right to choose when and how I spoke."

The officer asked if I wanted to come and talk to her about it, and I said yes. I knew that if the police were already involved, I needed to speak for myself. I had stayed silent for long enough, partly because I had been afraid and partly because I had been made to feel responsible for protecting everyone else from the truth.

I had to go back to Yorkshire to give the interview, and I took my best friend with me. My younger brother took us to the station. I was nervous, but having them there helped. It made me feel less alone walking into something so difficult.

The police officer I spoke to was lovely. She treated me with care and respect, and she stayed with me throughout the whole ordeal. That mattered more than she probably realised. When you have spent years expecting your pain to be dismissed or twisted, being treated gently can feel almost unfamiliar.

It took a year to get to court. That year was not easy. Even when you are not speaking about it every day, something like that sits in the background of your life. You know it is coming. You know there may be questions, statements, courtrooms, and memories you would rather not touch again.

Luckily, on the day the trial was supposed to start, my uncle admitted what he had done. That meant I did not have to go through the full trial. I was relieved because I do not know how I would have coped with having to relive everything in that way.

There was some justice in him admitting it, but there was also a strange sadness. Nothing about it felt victorious. It did not undo what happened. It did not give back the years I had spent carrying it quietly. It simply meant I did not have to fight as hard to be believed.

What made me so angry was the fact that my mother had persuaded me not to go to the police, then did it behind my back years later. She had stopped me when I was ready to speak, then spoke for me when it suited her. That is the part I struggle with most.

I do not believe she did it to get justice for me. I wish I could believe that. I wish I could look at it and see a mother finally standing up for her daughter. But that is not how it felt. It felt like control. It felt like another way of proving that she could still make decisions around my life, even after I had not spoken to her for five years.

At that point, I had built distance from her. I was no longer living with her. I had reconnected with my dad. I had begun to understand more of the truth about my life. Yet somehow, she still managed to insert herself into something that should have been mine to handle in my own time.

Reporting the abuse should have been about me. It should have been about what happened, what I survived, and what I was ready to say. Instead, it became tangled up with my mother again. Her anger. Her timing. Her need to be involved.

Still, I did speak. I went to the police. I gave the interview. I faced what had happened, even though the choice had not begun in the way it should have. That matters to me now. She may have tried to take control of the situation, but in the end, my voice was still the one that told the truth.

For years, I had been quiet because I was afraid of what the truth would do to everyone else. This time, even through anger and hurt, I finally said what had been done to me. That was not easy, but it was mine.

Chapter 15
The Loss of a Wonderful Man

After everything I had been through, my dad had become one of the safest people in my life. He was not perfect because nobody is, but he was kind, steady, gentle, and present in a way I had needed for so long. Losing him felt like losing the one person who had helped me understand what love was supposed to feel like.

"Some losses do not just break your heart. They take away the place where your heart finally felt safe."

After my dad passed away, I really struggled. He died before the sentencing for my uncle had taken place, so he never got to see what sentence he received. That was painful in itself, but the hardest part was that my dad had become everything to me at that time in my life.

I had spoken to him that morning before he left to go to his tennis match. It was an ordinary conversation, the kind you do not think too much about because you assume there will be another one later. I had no idea that would be the last time I spoke to him.

That is one of the cruellest parts of loss. You do not always know when the last moment is happening. You do not know to hold on tighter, say more, or remember every detail. Life just carries on as normal, until suddenly it does not.

My self-harm got worse after that. Two months later, my uncle was sentenced, and around that time, I took an overdose. I hated life. I felt completely alone, even though my half-brothers lived across the road and the youngest one came over to mine most days after our dad passed.

That is the strange thing about grief and depression. You can have people nearby and still feel unreachable inside yourself. I was surrounded by people who cared in their own ways, but the loss of my dad had opened something so deep in me that I could not seem to climb out of it.

I was angry, but mostly with myself. That had always been my pattern. I did not know how to be angry outwardly in a healthy way, so the anger turned back on me. I carried it in my body, in my thoughts, and in the way I punished myself for pain I did not know how to survive.

One night, I had truly given up on life. I could not see anything improving. I took an overdose, but then I panicked and called an ambulance. I do not really know why I called. I think some part of me must have still wanted to live, even if another part of me could not bear the pain anymore.

I was taken to hospital, and they called my mother because, without me realising it, she was still listed as my emergency contact. That felt like life pulling me back into something I had worked so hard to get away from. At one of the worst moments of my life, she was suddenly there again.

She said I was unconscious by the time I arrived at the hospital. She and both of my brothers came to see me, but unfortunately, that meant my mother was back in my life.

It felt as though she was almost enjoying being there. That may sound harsh, but that is honestly how it seemed. She always appeared to become energised when there were doctors, nurses, attention, and sympathy involved. It was as though my crisis gave her a role to play.

She also told me I was just like her because she had once tried to take her own life. The way she said it made me feel deeply uncomfortable, almost as though she was pleased by the comparison. I did not feel comforted by it. I felt pulled back into her story, as if even my lowest moment somehow had to become about her.

The hospital recommended that I go into a mental health unit, and I agreed. My mother visited me every day. She was staying at my house, which was about a half-hour drive away. Of course, she fitted in well and even made a friend in the unit.

I was only there for two weeks because my mother said she would take care of me, so they allowed me to leave in her care. Looking back, that feels painful and almost unbelievable. The person I had spent so much of my life trying to survive was now being trusted to care for me.

At the time, I was too broken and exhausted to fight much of anything. I needed help, but I did not yet know how to insist on the right kind of help.

I was only in contact with my mother for about six months after that. The last time I spoke to her, we were at her house. She told me I was as manipulative as my uncle, the same uncle who had abused me as a child. Then she stormed upstairs.

I do not even remember saying anything that would explain such a cruel reaction. I just remember sitting there afterwards, stunned and hurt. I stayed for about thirty to forty-five minutes before I found the courage to leave.

One of the cats was sitting on my lap. I picked her up, hugged her goodbye, and then I left. There was something heartbreaking about that moment. Saying goodbye to the cat felt easier than saying goodbye to my mother because the cat had never made me feel cruel, guilty, or unsafe.

It was two in the morning when I walked back to my car. As I was leaving, my mother texted me saying, "Get home safe, love you."

That message made everything feel even more twisted. She had just compared me to the man who abused me, then sent a message that sounded loving. That kind of emotional whiplash was something I had known my whole life, but that night, I could not carry it anymore.

When I got home, I took another overdose. This time, I did not ring anyone. Somehow, I woke up. I had been sick, which I believe is what saved me.

I have not spoken to my mother in ten years, and I will not speak to her again. She is far too toxic for me to have in my life. That decision did not come from hatred. It came from survival. There are some people you have to love from a distance, or not at all, because being close to them costs too much of yourself.

Losing my dad nearly destroyed me. Letting my mother back in nearly did too. But that final moment with her became a line I could not cross again. I had already lost so much. I could not keep losing myself as well.

Chapter 16
Grandparents Who Helped Me Survive

This is the last chapter of my story, and I do not want it to end only with pain. My life has held a great deal of hurt, but it has also held love. Not always from the places it should have come from, and not always in the ways I needed at the time, but it was there. My grandparents were a big part of that.

They gave me something steady when so much of my childhood felt uncertain. They fed us, loved us, welcomed us, and made weekends feel warmer than the rest of the week often did. I do not know how we would have managed without them.

My grandparents have always played a huge part in my life. Without their love, their endless support, and, of course, the lovely meals they gave us every weekend, I honestly do not know how we would have survived. Their home was one of the few places that felt reliable. We knew we would be fed there. We knew we would be welcomed there. We knew, in our own way, that they cared.

In the letter my mother wrote to me, she made out that I had chosen straightening my hair and seeing friends over visiting my grandparents. That was not true. There was one occasion when I said I would like to go out with my friends because they were going to pick me up from my grandparents' house. My mother was annoyed by that, but my grandmother was perfectly happy to let me see them.

I was seventeen years old, and my grandmother respected that. She understood that I loved them, but that I also wanted to see my friends. That is a normal part of being young. Wanting a social life did not mean I loved my grandparents any less.

We spent every weekend at my grandparents' house and had done since I was very young. They were not people I avoided. They were people I loved deeply. My mother twisting that into something else was hurtful, but it was not surprising. She often took one small moment and turned it into a version of events that suited her.

It happened once, but in my mother's eyes, it became proof of something awful. What I find strange is that my older brother often saw friends instead of going to our grandparents, and she never seemed to have a problem with that. But when I did it once, it became a big deal. In her letter, she made it sound as though I clearly did not love my grandparents, which is an absolute lie.

They mean everything to me, and they always have.

I believe I got my fighting spirit from my grandmother, although I do wish I had more of her confidence. She does not let anyone tell her to do anything she does not want to do. I have always admired that about her. She has a strength that feels natural, the kind of strength that does not need to shout to be real.

I would love to be more like that. In some ways, maybe I am learning to be.

"Healing has not meant forgetting. It has meant finally choosing myself."

One day, when I was being tested at hospital to find out why I could not feel my legs, the receptionist asked if my emergency contact was still my mother. I panicked a bit because I had not realised I had never changed it.

That one question brought back such a strong reaction. After everything, the thought of my mother being contacted again in a crisis frightened me. Thankfully, my emergency contact is now my husband. That may sound like a simple change, but to me it felt important. It was another way of making sure my life no longer led back to her.

It turned out that I have MS. As difficult as that diagnosis was, I was relieved to finally know what was wrong. It is awful when something is clearly not right with your body, but you have no idea what it is. Having a name for it helped.

I was also relieved that my emergency contact had been changed. It felt like one more piece of control being placed back into my own hands.

I have had to work very hard to become truly happy. My dad helped a great deal with that, and so did the counsellor I saw after he passed away. I have seen three counsellors in my life, but she was by far the best. She was the one who truly helped me.

She also told me that it was my own hard work that helped me move through the trauma. I think I needed to hear that. For so long, I had felt weak, damaged, or somehow behind everyone else. Hearing that I had worked hard to heal helped me see myself differently.

Healing did not happen because time passed. It happened because I faced things I had spent years trying not to feel.

I was desperate not to end up as miserable as my mother. That gave me a strong reason to do whatever work was necessary. I did not want bitterness to become my whole personality. I did not want pain to turn me into someone who hurt other people because I had been hurt.

The memories of my past have not disappeared. I do not think they ever fully will. But they do not control me in the same way anymore. I can think about them now without feeling as though I am still trapped inside them. That, to me, is progress.

I am finally truly happy, and I do not say that lightly. Happiness did not come easily to me. I had to build it slowly, with help, honesty, boundaries, and a lot of painful work.

I have come to terms with the fact that my mother will never apologise for how she treated me. I believe she truly thinks she has done nothing wrong. Waiting for an apology from someone like that only keeps you tied to them.

Once I accepted that the apology was not coming, I was finally able to move on with my life. That does not mean what happened was okay. It does not mean I have forgotten. It simply means I stopped waiting for her to become the mother I needed her to be.

I hope my story helps others who are still in a situation like this, or who have come out of one, to see that life can still turn out okay. Happiness is possible, even after years of pain. It may not happen quickly, and it may not look the way expected, but it can happen.

It took my third counsellor for me to find someone who truly fit, someone I felt comfortable opening up to completely. I completed the sessions with the other two, but my last counsellor was amazing. She helped me in a way I will always be grateful for.

I would say to anyone carrying trauma: finding the right person to talk to matters. It has to be someone safe, someone comfortable, someone who allows the truth to come out without shame. Speaking about trauma is difficult, but keeping it buried can hurt for far longer.

It took me years to understand that talking about what happened was not weakness. It was part of taking my life back.

What happened to me will always be part of my story, but it does not define all of me. For a long time, I thought my past had shaped me into someone broken beyond repair. I do not believe that anymore. I was hurt, deeply hurt, but I was not destroyed.

Healing has not meant forgetting. It has not meant pretending any of it was okay. It has meant facing the truth, grieving what I lost, and choosing to build something better for myself. It has meant learning that I am allowed to have boundaries. I am allowed to say no. I am allowed to protect my peace.

There are still moments when the past creeps in. Certain memories still hurt. Some losses will always ache, especially the years I lost with my dad and the time I wish I could have had with him. But those memories no longer control me the way they once did.

I have a husband who loves me. I have people in my life who truly care. I have learned to trust my own voice, even after years of being made to doubt it. I have learned that love should not feel like fear, that family is not always defined by blood, and that walking away from someone toxic is not cruelty. Sometimes it is survival.

My life is not perfect, but it is mine now. That means more to me than I can ever fully explain. After years of being controlled, blamed, silenced, and made to feel small, I finally have a life that belongs to me.

I survived my childhood. I survived my mother. I survived grief, trauma, self-harm, and the long road back to myself.

Now, I am not just surviving anymore. I am living. That is the ending I never thought I would have.